The Sun is Your Father

A Castle Family History

by

Sandra E. Baker

❧ Reciprocity Publishing, Victoria BC, Canada

The Sun is Your Father: A Castle Family History

"[Sophie] vaguely remembered seeing a strange man with red hair coming to her home, but didn't know he was there to arrange for her to go to a boarding school for girls in the nearby hamlet of Yale. In later years, she learned that the redheaded man, named Robert Kennedy, was her father."

These unusual Castle family life stories are of my grandmother and her first three children, spanning over 100 years (1890-1998). The children were not of Indian status but were sent to live at an Indian residential school, named Coqualeetza Industrial Institute. What was so unusual was that my mother loved her school, but her siblings had different experiences.

Published in Canada by Reciprocity Publishing, Victoria BC Canada
www.reciprocitypublishing.com   rev: 2021-08-01
ISBN: 978-1-928114-32-1 (softcover)

APA Citation: Baker, S. E. (2020). *The sun is your father: A Castle family history*. Reciprocity Publishing: Victoria BC.

Library and Archives Canada Cataloguing in Publication

Title: The sun is your father : a Castle family history / by Sandra E. Baker.
Names: Baker, Sandra E., 1939- author.
Description: Includes bibliographical references.
Identifiers: Canadiana 20200324586 | ISBN 9781928114321 (softcover)
Subjects: LCSH: Andrews, Sophie, 1890-1965. | LCSH: Andrews, Sophie, 1890-1965—Family. | LCSH:
    Castle, Ruth, 1912-1994. | LCSH: Castle, Ruth, 1912-1994—Family. |
    LCSH: Indigenous peoples—
    Education—British Columbia—Chilliwack—History—20th century. |
    LCSH: Indigenous peoples—British Columbia—Biography. | LCSH:
    Coqualeetza Industrial Institute (Chilliwack, B.C.) |
    LCSH: Coqualeetza Residential School (Chilliwack, B.C.) |
    CSH: Indigenous peoples—British Columbia—Chilliwack—Residential
    schools. | LCGFT: Biographies.
Classification: LCC E96.6.C67 B35 2020 | DDC 971.1004/9700922—dc23

Praise for The Sun is Your Father...

An incredible story of one family's journey through the residential school system in British Columbia. The author gives us a unique insight into her Indigenous roots dating back to the gold rush of the 1860s. A story filled with historical information and surprising facts.

-- George Reynolds

The Sun Is Your Father is an excellent read about a family's triumph over potential adversity. The stories about Ruth's family interactions are delightful. It was a pleasure to learn about Ruth's positive experience at Coqualeetza Residential school and her work with First Nations people, first as secretary and then editor of The Native Voice in the mid 1940s. Coqualeetza was an exceptional residential school educating two generations of land claims leaders, including Peter Kelly, chair of the Allied tribes (1916-1927) and Frank Calder, lead plaintiff in the landmark Calder case in 1973.

--John McLeod

A very enjoyable and educational read. It was interesting to learn how the Castle children's lives progressed during and after they left school. So many of us knew nothing about what was happening to the First Nations children. The author has done a wonderful job in her research of family history and Coqualeetza Residential School.

-- Marilyn Linton

Contents

Family Tree

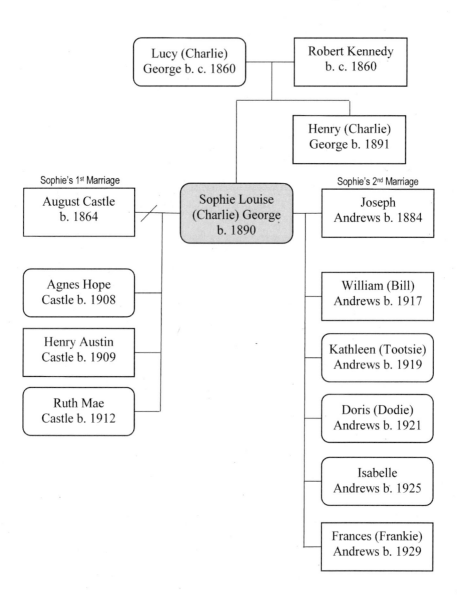

Lucy (Charlie) George b. c. 1860 — Robert Kennedy b. c. 1860

Henry (Charlie) George b. 1891

Sophie's 1st Marriage

August Castle b. 1864

Sophie Louise (Charlie) George b. 1890

Sophie's 2nd Marriage

Joseph Andrews b. 1884

Agnes Hope Castle b. 1908

Henry Austin Castle b. 1909

Ruth Mae Castle b. 1912

William (Bill) Andrews b. 1917

Kathleen (Tootsie) Andrews b. 1919

Doris (Dodie) Andrews b. 1921

Isabelle Andrews b. 1925

Frances (Frankie) Andrews b. 1929

Preface

When my sister and I were young children, we were unaware that our mother, Ruth Castle, and her two older siblings, Hope and Henry, had lived their entire school years in an Indian[1] residential school (1915-1931). The school, named Coqualeetza Industrial Institute, was located in Sardis, British Columbia (B.C.), just outside of Chilliwack.

Ruth's school-day memories were mainly happy ones, but her experiences were comparatively different than that of Hope's and Henry's. Unlike other residential schools, there were few known horror stories of abuse at Coqualeetza, mainly because of its principal, Reverend George W. Raley, (also known as Dr. Raley). He had great respect for B.C.'s Indigenous people and he offered a diverse education for the children, in comparison to other residential schools. He had studied and worked with various tribes in B.C. for over thirty years before receiving his position at Coqualeetza.

Dr. Raley spoke on CBC radio in 1945 telling of the philosophy of the totem and history of British Columbia's Indian people. His entire speech is copied in Chapter 6.

---

[1] **NOTE:** Indigenous people were referred to as "Indians" during the time period of these stories and the term is therefore used throughout this book.

The name of this book is from the first line of a prayer that was taught to the Coqualeetza children.

Our grandmother and the Castle children's mother, Sophie, was born in 1890. She also spent her childhood in a boarding school, named All Hallows of the West, located in Yale, B.C. This school originated as a school for native Indian girls but later became known as a young ladies' finishing school for white girls. Both Coqualeetza and All Hallows were Anglican residential schools and both were unique.

When my mother died in 1994, she left a treasured box of newspaper clippings, school annuals, photographs, and some of her writings she had saved as material for a book she and a few of her school friends had intended to write in the 1970s about their beloved Coqualeetza. The book was to incorporate the history of the school and how it affected the lives of various students.

Ruth and one of her school friends, Delvina (nicknamed Dolly), travelled to Vancouver Island and other B.C. areas to interview their old school friends from Coqualeetza. The interviews were tape-recorded and filed away in her box of book material.

Ruth and Dolly's experiences at school were generally happy ones. Having English as their first language was a great advantage for them at Coqualeetza. Dolly was from a native Indian family and her parents and family were from the Sardis area where English was prevalent. Since Ruth's two older siblings were already living at Coqualeetza, she was anxious to leave home and move to Coqualeetza with them, even at the age of four. Also, she was not leaving a happy environment at home.

After travelling and collecting information for the book, Ruth and Dolly began to question the idea of actually having their book published. By this time, so much new information had surfaced about the brutal treatment of Indian children in other residential schools, they decided to put their book aside.

After my Uncle Henry died in 1998, the last of the three siblings to die, I suddenly felt compelled to write their stories. Since I possessed my mother's box of material, but do not have her acquired knowledge of Coqualeetza or know the Indian people she loved so deeply, I chose to write the book in a different context — to focus on portions of Sophie's and her first three children's lives, during and after their school years. I have included brief histories of their schools, as these schools were their actual childhood homes and had a great effect on their entire lives.

Hope, Henry and Ruth were half native Indian but were not born into an Indian culture; therefore, their experiences cannot be compared to most other residential school survivors. They were not of legal Indian Status, nor were they required to live under the rules of the Federal Indian Act in order to keep their Indian Status rights, so they went on to live their lives as other Canadians citizens.

During the beginning of 2001, I studied my mother's much-treasured box of material for her book, interviewed many family members, and took several research trips to Ashcroft, Yale, Sardis, Vancouver and Vancouver Island.

After filtering through the material, I was surprised how some of the family stories I had heard over the years began to surface. I greatly relied on the cooperation of other family members' recollections and research for this information. Coincidentally, my cousin, Doreen, (Hope's daughter), recently researched the family history and put together books of official documents, writings, photos and articles. This information, and her enthusiasm for this project, have been invaluable to me.

Hope, Henry, and Ruth maintained their deep-rooted bonds originating from their childhood. They were born near the beginning of the twentieth century and all died near the end. Their lives took place mainly in and around the areas of British Columbia shown on the map following.

Trans Canada Highway (Fraser Canyon)

Part One

Chapter One: Sophie

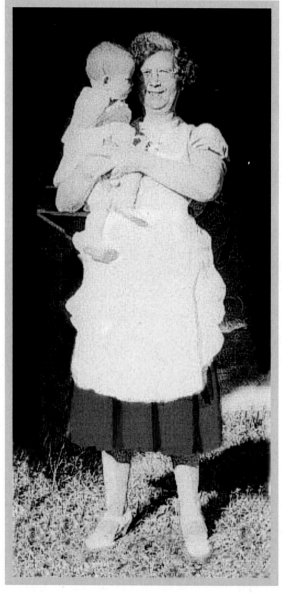

Sophie and me, 1940

G randma Sophie and I got along beautifully. She lived with us in Vancouver in the 1940s when my sister and I were children. I loved to help her in the garden and we would listen to all the radio shows together. We both especially loved The Lone Ranger and never missed an episode. She would sit in her rocking chair, knitting and embroidering, while we listened and enjoyed.

Sophie usually wore a starched, white apron over a traditional navy skirt, white blouse, sensible Cuban-heeled shoes and nylon stockings. She kept her room sparkling clean, always with frilly white curtains. I saved her autograph in my autograph book and admired her rounded, English-style handwriting. She wrote:

Dec 10, 1948

As sure as grass
Grows around a stump
You are my darling Sugarlump
Grandma

My sister and I knew nothing about our grandma's childhood. She seemed like everyone else's grandma in our white, middle-class neighbourhood of Kitsilano in Vancouver. If we had asked her about it, she probably would not have told us that she was raised in an Indian girls' boarding school. Because of the times, being

Indian, or even part Indian, was considered shameful to many and often kept hushed. There is so much we will never know about Sophie.

Until Sophie was four years old, she lived with her family in Pop'kw'em (Popkum), a small Indian village in the Stó:lō Nation territory near Chilliwack, B.C. She vaguely remembered seeing a strange man with red hair coming to her home but didn't know he was there to arrange for her to go to a boarding school for girls in the nearby hamlet of Yale. In later years, she learned that the redheaded man, named Robert Kennedy, was her father.

Sophie's mother, Lucy Charlie, was born during the time of the great British Columbia gold rush in 1860, just before the smallpox epidemic swept the province and killed much of the native Indian population. The epidemic started in the Victoria area in 1862 (originating from San Francisco) and spread rapidly up the northern coast and into the B.C. interior.

In his book, *British Columbia's Disasters*, writer-historian Derek Pethick, wrote:

> The *Colonist* [Victoria newspaper] made a
> sober assessment of the dimensions of the
> tragedy: "How have the mighty fallen! Four
> short years ago, numbering their braves by
> thousands, they were the scourge and terror of
> the coast. ... What were our philanthropists

about, that they were not up the coast ahead of the disease two months ago, engaged in vaccinating the poor wretches who have since fallen victims? Who among our missionaries will volunteer to save the aborigines from utter extermination?" On July 7 [1862] the *Colonist* declared: "The northerners as tribes are now nearly exterminated. They have disappeared from the face of this fair earth at the approach of the pale-face, as snow melts beneath the rays of the noonday sun."

In the interior, too, the epidemic took its dreadful toll. A letter from a missionary to Governor Douglas gave some idea of the disaster: "The native population around Lillooet have for the last two months been suffering under the visitation of smallpox. This disease has made fearful ravages amongst them, sweeping off whole families, and literally converting their camps into graveyards.

Events in the Cariboo, where one of the greatest gold rushes in history was at its peak, received at least as much space in the press as the smallpox. A letter from a miner to a friend in Victoria, first appeared at this time in the *Colonist*: "I am well and so are all the rest of the boys. I avail myself of the present

opportunity to write you half a dozen lines to
let you know that I am well and doing well –
making from two to three thousand dollars a
day! Times good – grub high – whiskey bad –
money plenty."

It is estimated that when the 19th century
opened, there were about 80,000 Indians in
what is now British Columbia…. So great was
the disruption of their culture that, even when
the epidemic had largely spent its force, the
population continued to decline. By 1885 it fell
to about 28,000.

Canoes eventually yielded to large paddle wheelers on
the Fraser River and Yale became highly disreputable,
crowded with railroaders and gold miners. Many Stó:lō
women were taken as temporary *Indian Wives* (meaning
not officially married) by gold miners who had no
intention of staying in the territory once they had collected
their gold.

An excerpt from the book, *You Are Asked to Witness,*
by Keith Thor Carlson, states:

A British journalist with the *London Times*
reported from the gold fields near Yale that the
"Indians complain that the whites abuse them
sadly, take their squaws away, shoot their
children, and take their salmon by force." In

the opinion of the reporter, "some of the 'whites' are sad dogs."

Missionaries soon arrived on the notorious trail of gold rush towns, on quests to save sinful souls, and several Anglicans were sent to the village of Popkum to build the Saint Maria Magdalene Church. One of the missionaries was a lumberman, named Robert Kennedy. It is doubtful, but not known, if Lucy was smitten with Kennedy, but Lucy soon became Kennedy's Indian wife. It was widely known that Indian women were used and often abused by some powerful church and other officials, and also by travelling prospectors.

On February 3, 1890, Lucy gave birth to Sophie Louise, a healthy, plump, fair-skinned baby. Shortly after the birth of Sophie, Lucy was pregnant once again. In January 1891, a boy, she named Henry, was born.

The relationship between Lucy Charlie and Robert Kennedy did not last. After the completion of the church building, Kennedy left Popkum to work in other areas, returning to Popkum only occasionally. He had married an Irish woman in Chilliwack on September 15, 1890, the same year Sophie was born. By 1892, Lucy married a local Indian man, named Harry George. Lucy and her children then changed their last name from Charlie to George.

Two years later, when Sophie was four years old, Robert Kennedy took it upon himself to register her in the residential school for girls in Yale, called All Hallows of the West, where she would obtain an English education by well-respected Anglican nuns from England.

~oo0oo~

Chapter Two:
All Hallows of the West

Procession goes to Chapel

All Hallows of the West, c. 1890

In 1884, when the gold rush boom had begun to pass, Bishop Sillitoe, the first bishop of the diocese of New Westminster, was convinced that a school for Indian girls was essential to carry out God's work. He sent for three nuns from the Order of All Hallows in Ditchington, Norfolk, England, (his original home), to take on the task of running the school — to be named, All Hallows of the West. These nuns were cultured, well-educated women from a proper, upper-class environment. It was probably an enormous culture shock for them to arrive in a place like Yale, having to walk past the red-light district, gambling parlours, and a dozen saloons full of drunken men.

In only a few instances were Indian children in Canada allowed to attend the white children's schools. For an Indian child to receive a formal English education, the child would be required to live away from home in an Indian residential school. It was not yet compulsory for Indian children to attend a residential school, but a child could be registered at the request of a representative of the church or taken from or given up by a dislocated family.

There was virtually no funding for the education of Indian children by the federal government, and very little funding was available for the All Hallows school by the Anglican Church, so the nuns more or less had to fend for themselves by seeking donations and taking in washing.

Yale was so crowded in 1884 that the nuns had to start the school in the vicarage, adjacent to the Anglican Church, (St. John the Divine). This church is the oldest church still standing in B.C. It was originally built by Anglicans to civilize the miners. Exhibits within the church today include original altar pieces from the 1860s as well as a collection of antique linens, many hand-stitched by the students of All Hallows.

A solution for All Hallows' financial problem came when the New Westminster's Columbian College for white girls collapsed financially. The nuns agreed to take on the white girls' schooling, which had been financed by pupil fees and funds promised to the college by an English missionary society. They purchased Brookside, the spacious, palatial home and grounds formerly occupied by the famous railroad contractor, Andrew Onderdonk, who had built the railway through the Fraser Canyon.

By the time Sophie arrived at All Hallows in 1894, white girls were the majority and it had become known as a high-end finishing school. Many white girls were missionaries' daughters or were from upper-class families of prominent local government officials, railway officials or wealthy prospectors. Some had fathers known as Indian Fighters.

Artist's rendition of Front Street, Yale, B.C.
(entitled Payday Yale)

Front Street in Yale, 1882
Business establishments fronting the Fraser River

Front Street, July 2002

When Sophie arrived at All Hallows at only four years old, she was afraid of the nuns in their hooded black capes who spoke a language she didn't understand. They were not similar in any way to the warm, loving people she knew, and she longed to go home to her family. Years later, however, she revealed that she absolutely loathed one family member — her stepfather, Harry George. She said he inflicted unspeakable abuse on her, and she carried this burdensome secret with her for many years. The resentment she felt towards him was so strong it ultimately destroyed her relationship with her mother, Lucy. It is not known how frequently Lucy visited Sophie at All Hallows, but her visits eventually stopped.

Sophie might have been mistaken for a white girl, having pale skin like her father, but there would never be that mistake made — Indian girls were in the Indian School section, separate from the Canadian School for white girls. Bishop Sillitoe assured prospective English parents that the white girls would be treated in a manner consistent with their station in life. The church magazine reported that, at the request of the English parents, the Canadian girls were not to be mixed with the Indian girls and they were instructed to not even *look* at the Indian girls. The only time they saw each other was during services in the chapel — Indian girls on one side in red caps and pinafores, white girls in white dresses and white veils on the other. The nuns referred to girls in both schools as 'daughters' and all the students referred to each other as 'sisters'.

Unlike the Canadian girls, the Indian girls were required to perform half work days. They rose an hour earlier than the Canadian girls in order to do housework before the chapel service at 7:30 a.m. Their other domestic duties were interspersed during the school day, which included performing another hour of kitchen and dining room jobs while the Canadian girls dressed for dinner.

Both schools had strict rules to follow and there were all the usual discomforts of the times. For example, it was common for the air in the schools to be full of smoke from the stovepipes and in the winter their washbasins would often have a thin covering of ice in the morning.

The nuns censored outgoing and incoming letters but some of the more daring girls used the secret rock outside where a non-student neighbour would collect their uncensored letters to mail.

The following rules were posted on the wall of the Canadian School:

Short Rules for Comfort at Home

- Put self first.
- Be prompt at every meal.
- Take little annoyances out of the way.
- When any good happens to anyone, rejoice.
- When anyone suffers, drop a word of sympathy.
- Tell of your own faults rather than those of others.
- Have a place for everything and everything in its place.
- Hide your own troubles, but watch to help others out of theirs.
- Never interrupt any conversation, but wait patiently your turn to speak.
- Look for beauty in everything, and take a cheerful view of every event.
- Always speak kindly and politely to servants.
- When inclined to give an angry answer, press your lips together, and say the alphabet.

Irene Bjerky, the great granddaughter of one of the Indian School girls, Clara Dominic, wrote the following passages:

The two schools had extremely different curriculums, though of course both studied Scripture, reading and writing. In the Canadian School the white girls, uniformed in navy blue during the week and clad in white dresses with violet sashes on Sundays, studied advanced subjects such as English literature, arithmetic, history, geography, music, art, drama, Natural Science, and French, German and Latin. Matriculation of University Entrance examinations were given by McGill University.

The girls of the Indian school, dressed in plain brown dresses during the week and print dresses with red pinafores and beanies for Sunday, studied and received prizes for such practical skills as needle-work, bread-making, housework, laundry-work, cleanliness, and conduct. They were not expected to need any higher education. Marriage to a white man was aspiration enough, it seemed.

The following extracts are from passages describing Clara Dominic's last Christmas at All Hallows. She was to marry a white man, Frank Clare, on Dec. 29' 1902.

The passages indicate that the anticipation of the imminent wedding caused much joy and excitement for the Indian School girls that Christmas season. They would enjoy teasing her, calling her Clara Clare, her soon-to-be married name.

Clara & William Frank Clare
December 29, 1902

[Christmas] was the only time of the year the Indian School was invited to the dining hall of the Canadian School, and all of the white girls had gone home to their families.

[Clara's] family had attended the services that Christmas Eve, coming all the way from Spuzzum on the train, and she had given extra thanks for their presence, their support, and their sharing in her last Christmas at All Hallows. The Christmas Tree party was the social peak of the Christmas season at All Hallows, and her husband-to-be had been in attendance. Frank had been lovely that day, witty and kind, and had charmed every one of her school sisters. He had been extremely polite when introduced to her mother Amelia and her sister Rhoda, gratifying and somewhat unusual in those days for a white man meeting Indian women.

Living at All Hallows created many close friendships for Sophie but she was desperately lonely for the love of her own family. Her brother, Henry, was her only family link, and she always looked forward to his rare visits. He was the only male in her life and she deeply admired him. This deep admiration lasted throughout her life and she spoke of him often.

Sophie acquired a mischievous and, at times, spiteful personality. The nuns would often look upon her when any kind of bad conduct or problems arose. But she did well in the academic work, had superb penmanship, and became an expert at the required 'womanly crafts'. She especially enjoyed learning music appreciation and reading Shakespeare. In later years, her children would love to hear her recite Shakespeare by heart, with a perfect English accent.

By the time Sophie was in her mid-teens, she became aware that the All Hallows girls were quite an attraction to some of the male population in Yale. She was apprehensive, but flattered, when she began receiving visits at the school from a well-known gentleman in the area, a railroader, named August Castle.

August had fine, English manners and charm, reserved especially for the ladies. He had a magnetic appeal many women apparently could not resist. How he came to know Sophie George is not known, but it is speculated that Sophie's uncle, (her mother's brother, Patrick Charlie, also a railroader), may have brought Sophie to August's attention.

Sophie was sixteen years old when August entered her life. When he visited her at All Hallows, they often devised ways to meet alone. A family member told me that she would sometimes jump the All Hallows fence late at night for their clandestine meetings. Sophie had a strong will and was intent on being with him. She may have been completely infatuated with August and believed he would give her the love and attention she craved, or he was just a way of escaping the school. We'll never know her true feelings about August at that time.

That same year, 1906, August received Lucy George's permission to permanently take her daughter, Sophie, from All Hallows.

The Church of St. John the Divine and Rectory, Yale, B.C., c. 1880

The Church of St. John the Divine, July 2002

All Hallows Canadian School Easter dress-up, 1905

All Hallows Canadian School students (autographed), 1906

One of the first photos of All Hallows Indian students and staff,
c. 1886

All Hallows Indian School girls, c. 1906
(Sophie is circled)

Article filed in Yale Archives:

By 1908, admissions to All Hallows Canadian School increased by leaps and bounds with girls coming from other provinces and several American states. It was an honour and a high point in the school's history when, in October 1901, it was visited by the Duke and Duchess of York (grandparents of the present Queen Elizabeth). As the school became more affluent, tennis and basketball courts, hockey and croquet greens were added. It apparently was not just a status symbol but also the quality of the higher education that made the school successful. The school's growing popularity resulted in more alternatives for this type of school, such as Vancouver's Crofton House School.

In 1918, All Hallows Indian School closed due to lack of funding and the Indian girls were sent to St. George's Residential School in Lytton. Two years later, All Hallows Canadian School closed because of dwindling registrations. Today no trace of All Hallows can be found, with the exception of a single road sign.

Photo of All Hallows road sign, July 2002

Following are excerpts from an article printed in a B.C. Historical News magazine entitled: *Lost Opportunity: All Hallows School for Indian and White Girls, 1884 – 1920,* written by author/historian, Jean Barman:

As the school grew with the admission of more and more white boarders, the Indian girls became responsible for all the household duties. As summed up by a white pupil: "They were the servants: they did the work." The only work activities performed by the Canadian girls appear to have been making their beds each morning after chapel and darning their stockings on Friday evening.

As the only school across Canada enrolling both Indian and white girls in the same facilities, [All Hallows] held the promise of bringing together two races during the critical years of the late-nineteenth century. The opportunity was lost. All Hallows never fulfilled its potential, and its failure to do so provides useful insights into both the school itself and the larger society in which it functioned.

~oo0oo~

Chapter Three:
An Indian Wife

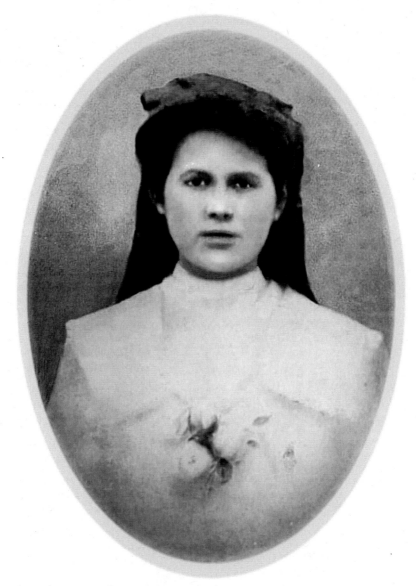

Sophie Louise George, age 16, 1906

It was a drastic and frightening change for Sophie to leave All Hallows and begin life with August Castle. She was now exposed to all the unruly, hard-drinking people she had previously seen only under the nuns' supervision or from behind the protective gates of All Hallows. August was the foreman of the track-laying crew for the Canadian Pacific Railway and she lived and traveled with him on a railroad car. Her job was to care for August's needs and perform kitchen and cleaning duties. She was required to sleep in a converted railroad car, called The Bunkhouse, with August and other C.P.R. employees.

August was a number of years older than Sophie — in fact, a shocking twenty-six years older. Besides being a C.P.R. employee, he was a prospector, and, at times, a posse leader hired to capture railroad bandits, including the now-famous Bill Miner.

When August was thirteen years old, he travelled with his brother from the coast to Yale by paddle wheeler after the sudden death of their parents in Victoria. Their father, Martin Cassel (later changed to Castle), emigrated from England; their mother, Jinni Eitan, was a native Indian from the Victoria area. It was said that their deaths were caused by a murder-suicide. Records of correspondence from Martin Cassel indicate that he was deeply distressed from the failure of his bakery businesses. He later burned them down, then shot Jinni and himself.

August Castle
(date unknown)

August was known as a great ladies' man, attractted to younger women. He was a widower with seven children from his second marriage; two were stepchildren. His eldest daughter was Sophie's age and may have attended All Hallows.

There was no wedding for Sophie, like Clara Clare's happy, celebratory wedding. Sophie did not call herself Mrs. Castle, and did not expect others to. She was realistic in her expectations and did her best to perform her required duties — cooking, cleaning, and being August's Indian wife, of sorts.

Since there were many members of August's family living in the Yale area, some were outwardly disapproving of young Sophie George. She felt extremely uncomfortable in her new role but hid her feelings well and conducted herself with an appearance of an uncaring attitude.

Within months, Sophie's opinion of August had completely dwindled. He would often abandon her to go on adventures, leaving her to stay with his brother or one of his friends in Yale. She became lonely and missed the companionship of her All Hallows sisters and warmth of her favourite teacher, Sister Agnes. She attended every possible service she could at her church, the Church of St. John the Divine, hoping her faith would help her through those lonely, miserable days. She soon faced the bleak reality of her life. She knew she had to stay with August; there was nowhere else for her to go.

On April 3, 1908, Sophie delivered a baby girl in the Ruby Creek Hospital. She was named, Agnes Hope. Sophie was small in stature, just over five feet tall, and was not prepared for the long, painful process of delivering a full-term baby. It was then that she wished she had emotional support from her mother or, least of all, August.

A portion of Hope's baptismal record, on deposit in the Archives of the Anglican Diocese of New Westminster, reads:

Child's Name:	143 Agnes Hope
Parent's Name:	Sophie Indian girl

Hope was beautiful and healthy with black hair and olive skin. She was a quiet, contented baby and Sophie soon began to feel the pleasure and sentiment of nursing and holding her. She hoped August would begin to show her some consideration and not continue keeping company with his rowdy friends. She loathed the atmosphere when they were present. They consumed vast amounts of alcohol and always ignored her pleas for peace and quiet. Because of Sophie's All Hallows' upbringing, August's friends would often make fun of her, imitating the way she spoke, and calling her stuck-up. She tried speaking back, using their bad grammar and foul language, but August would not allow it.

Within a year of Hope's birth, Sophie was expecting another child. On September 7, 1909, a boy, Henry Austin, was born. She chose to have this birth attended by a mid-wife, not in the Ruby Creek Hospital. Although Sophie did not want another child with August, she was pleased to have a son. She had always planned to name her first son Henry, after her much-loved brother.

A year after little Henry's birth, Sophie received the news of her mother's death. She knew little of Lucy George's life or how she died. According to the death certificate, she died of "unknown causes." A portion of the death certificate on deposit in the Archives of the Anglican Diocese, reads:

Name:	Lucy George
Age Next Birthday:	About 50 yrs.
Trade or Profession:	Indian woman

Lucy George (date unknown)

Henry George (Sophie's brother), c. 1911

Sophie attended Lucy's burial service at the Indian Cemetery in Yale but did not feel overcome with grief; she had been estranged from her mother too long. Her brother, Henry, was by her side for the service and she was thankful he was there.

Henry George had become an engineer for the C.P.R. and Sophie would always speak of him with great admiration and respect. As often as she could, she and the children traveled in the bunkhouse car with August to see Henry at his home in Revelstoke. When she learned that Henry's Danish wife disapproved of her, she was highly disturbed but could mask her feelings well. She put on a proud face, never revealing just how upsetting this was to her.

After the birth of her children, Sophie spent much of her time living in August's brother's cabin in Yale. She became friends with August's nephew, Joseph Andrews, who occasionally traveled to Yale from Vancouver to visit family members. He had befriended Sophie and considered August (his Uncle Gus) to be a formidable character.

Joseph Andrews was proud that his late father, Joseph Andrew Comeyne, was a whale hunter and fisherman from Hawaii. He had fished near Vancouver Island where he met Ellen Castle, August's sister. Unlike August, Ellen stayed on the reserve near Victoria after their parents' deaths. Joseph Comeyne died tragically at sea (apparently after a night of heavy drinking) when Joseph was a young boy.

Joseph was Ellen Castle's and Joseph Comeyne's only child. He was not given his father's surname, Comeyne because the registrar for the baptismal certificate apparently could not decipher the name, Comeyne, (derived from the Hawaiian name, Kamai) and chose the father's more recognizable middle name, Andrew(s) for the baby's surname.

Joseph was much closer to Sophie's age and had also attended a residential school in Washington State. They had much in common and Sophie was rather attracted to him. He had fine, handsome features, kind, honest eyes, and a quiet, gentlemanly manner. In addition, he played the violin, guitar and mandolin and had a magnificent singing voice. He enjoyed performing in Sophie's presence and she was a most-appreciative listener. In Sophie's dreamed-up schemes to escape from August, she considered the thought of someday going to live in Vancouver and calling upon Joseph for help.

Sophie was always especially aware of August's unchanged, lusty ways. It did not surprise her when he often brought a woman, named Emma, home for meals, which Sophie was expected to cook. The rumours in Yale were that Emma was August's new traveling companion.

It has recently been discovered that there was another daughter born to Sophie and August. She was named Ellen Francis May (or Mae), born on August 1st, 1911. She died in October of the same year. There are apparently no official documents of this birth. Sophie and August's third child, Ruth Mae, was born on September 6, 1912. Sophie blamed the premature birth of this baby on her wretched life with August and she agonized at the thought of having to bear any more of his children. He was now physically and emotionally abusive to her and she was desperately afraid of him.

Ruth Mae's baptism record, on deposit in the Archives of the Anglican Diocese, reads:

Child's name:	178 Ruth Mae
Parent's Name:	Sophie, half-breed
	living with August Castle

By 1914, when Ruth was two years old, Sophie began making real plans to move out of Yale with the children. The resentment and frustration of living with August had built up enough spunk in her to take the first steps. But she was penniless and would first have to start searching for work. She learned of a job opportunity as a clerk at the Yale Court House. This was a well-respected position and her education from All Hallows qualified her to be hired. She registered Hope in grade one at the Yale public school, found child-care for Ruth and Henry, and began her new job.

One Sunday, after attending church with the children, Sophie met Reverend George Raley, a kindly Methodist missionary. Reverend Raley learned that Sophie had attended All Hallows and suggested that she send her children to the school that his church had set up for Indian children, called the Coqualeetza Industrial Institute. This school was located in Sardis, just outside of Chilliwack. It had a fine reputation and their education would be similar to hers. She filled in the registration papers for Hope and Henry for the 1915 school term and gave them to Reverend Raley.

When Hope had completed the grade one school term, Sophie packed up the children and traveled to Canoe where she had been hired as a farm worker for the summer. Later that summer, she heard of the typhoid epidemic in the area and found a way to travel to Lytton to nurse in the hospital. Although these were not the best circumstances to practice the nursing skills she had learned at All Hallows, she was grateful to have the experience. The children were forced to share a room with typhoid victims while she worked; there was nowhere else to put them. When the epidemic was over, she reluctantly carried out the next desperate step of her plan.

To slowly prepare Hope and Henry for Coqualeetza, she would often tell them of the advantages of living at Coqualeetza and how important it was to have a good education. She planned that once they were safely in school, she would pack up little Ruth, travel to Vancouver, and call upon Joseph to take them in.

On a September day in 1915, Sophie took Hope and Henry to Chilliwack by train. They then walked from the station to the children's new home in Sardis, the Coqualeetza Industrial Institute.

~oo0oo~

Chapter Four:
Coqualeetza, 'The
Cleansing Place'

Coqualeetza Industrial Institute

Coqualeetza **was the name of an Indian settlement** in the Fraser Valley, long before the white man came. There have been many versions of the meaning of the Stó:lō name, Coqualeetza, the Cleansing Place. One Stó:lō version, from the book entitled, *A Stó:lō-Coast Salish Historical Atlas.* "Coqualeetza, Legacies of Land Use" is a story that relates to the importance of spiritual power and the power of women over physical strength and personal greed. The legend tells of women and spiritual power cleansing the spirit of some greedy men, affirming respectful, harmonious relations between men and women. The book states:

> The early Methodist missionaries often manipulated the original meaning to reflect their own objectives. They did not recognize the spiritual significance of the act of cleansing, and Coqualeetza became 'the place of cleansing,' where savages would be cleansed in the light of civilization, education and Jesus Christ.

During the latter stages of the smallpox epidemic in the Fraser Valley, Methodist missionaries, Reverend Tate and his wife, portioned off an area in their home in Sardis and provided room and board for orphaned Indian children with the idea of starting a Christian school. They later expanded their house, took in more children, and Mrs. Tate became teacher, matron and cook. When the house burned down in 1881, they began plans for construction of an Indian residential school building and were eventually successful in obtaining funds to have a brick structure built on Vedder Road, named the Coqualeetza Industrial Institute.

Within a few years, Indian children were being sent to the Coqualeetza Institute from other areas, mainly Port Simpson, Kitimat and Skidegate. The church officials originally had difficulty in obtaining the property for the school site because of community objections. In fact, Mrs. Tate wrote this observation from one of the residents in the area, "She told me they were afraid to have this school in their district as they felt the Indian boys would overrun the premises, destroy their orchards and become a general nuisance."

An excerpt from the book, You Are Asked to Witness: The *Stó:lō* in Canada's Pacific Coast History, by Keith Thor Carlson, states:

> The idea of having children raised by foreigners in an isolated residential school was distressing for the Stó:lō. Initially, some Stó:lō parents (primarily ones from high status families) did not allow their children to attend. For this reason, in the early years (before the government made residential school attendance compulsory), a large proportion of Stó:lō

children who were taken by missionaries to either St. Mary's or Coqualeetza, were from low status families, orphans, or sick children.

Coqualeetza students and staff, c. 1910

It was said that some staff members were teachers who were unable to obtain employment elsewhere and a residential school was their last resort. Most of the female teachers were spinsters and many were missionaries with the highest of moral standards. The main requirement for the appointment of a principal was to be a good disciplinarian and Reverend Tate's official title was Moral Governor.

An early Coqualeetza teacher wrote:

I came on a June day soon after arriving in Canada from England in 1911. I was really rather terrified of the huge Indian youths, who were really difficult to control. One day when they were more than ordinarily unruly, I went to the teachers' dining room where breakfast was in progress, and cried in desperation to Miss Pitman, "Will you come?" Miss Pitman rose from the table, she entered the pupils' dining room. She didn't speak. She just stood there, and immediately there fell that silence that could be felt. Her greatest forte was as a stern disciplinarian, and both boys and girls were quelled immediately.

I, who had excellent testimonials from England as to my being a good disciplinarian, was as a candle to a searchlight compared with Miss Pitman. Moreover, the very size of those great lads whom I was supposed to chastise with a whip – but never could – intimidated me. But there came improvement later when the girls sent a note to the boys: "Please, boys, be kind to Miss G and Miss M."

Besides religious teachings, it was a program of half-work and half-school days. The half-school day included basics in the three R's but concentrated mainly on industrial training and farming for the boys and general housekeeping, cooking and sewing for the girls. Because of low funding for Indian residential schools, the farm work was not only for the purpose of supplying the school larder with food, but to sell some of their produce to generate more income for operating costs. Some students complained that the Haida children (considered to be the elite tribe) believed they should not have to perform the same work as the others.

A former student briefly described the work at school:

> We cleaned up the kitchen, did the baking of bread, the laundering, sewing and all the maintenance, grew our own fruits and vegetables, looked after the cows, horses, pigs and chickens. Before there was a nurse, school stopped if there was an epidemic of the measles or the chicken pox and the well students looked after the sick ones.

The Institute had extremely poor conditions. There was no indoor plumbing and the kitchen and dining area had constant problems with rats. There were not proper sleeping accommodations for most students; some boys were required to sleep in tents year-round. The classrooms were cold and many classes were held in tents with one or two board walls.

Following is just one portion of the many Rules for Boys set out by the Inspector for Indian Schools, 1906.

RULES [for boys]

To be repeated by pupils after tea, daily until understood; after which to be said on Wednesdays and Saturdays before prayers. These rules are to be explained, taught thoroughly and infractions of them are to be reported nightly.

1. We must always speak the truth.

2. We must never steal or touch others' things.

3. We must not use bad words.

4. We must keep the Sabbath holy.

5. We must pray to God both morning and evening.

6. We must be kind to each other.

7. We must be polite (salute properly, remove our hats indoors).

8. We must be clean and tidy.

9. We must be punctual.

10. We must be obedient to our officers and monitors.

11. We must work well and not idle or play in work hours.

12. We must not talk Indian (except when allowed).

13. We must not break bounds.

14. We must not wrestle or be rough indoors.

15. We must not talk loudly or be noisy indoors.

16. We must not go to dormitories in the day time.

17. We must not talk in bed, get in others' beds or leave the dormitories at night.

18. We must not smoke, chew gum or spit on the floors.

19. We must not write or receive letters secretly.

20. We must be careful of books and things we are trusted with.

21. We must not play with matches or fire.

22. We must not waste, harm or destroy anything.

23. We must be careful of windows.

24. We must be industrious and prepare ourselves to be good, useful men.

Religion was a central part of the students' daily lives; whistling on Sundays was not allowed and frivolous books or games were put away until Monday. An ex-student recalled:

> When I look back on Sundays at Coqualeetza I remember rising early, washing, brushing my teeth and saying morning prayers. Then at 11 o'clock, we attended the regular service, then the evening service. At the time, I thought that a kid coming out of Coqualeetza was already half way to heaven, they can't get into trouble now.

Reverend G. W. Raley

Reverend George W. Raley was appointed as principal of Coqualeetza in 1914. He was highly respected and trusted by Coqualeetza students and staff and it was said he would personally conduct a fire inspection of the entire school every night at midnight. He had a deep interest in Indian culture and was a devoted collector of Indian art. Because times were hard, he was appointed "to give the place a decent burial," he said, years later. But his long experience in Indian work had prepared him well for what would be the resurrection of Coqualeetza.

~oo0oo~

Chapter Five:
An English Education

Coqualeetza Staff, 1910

In 1977, Hope briefly described her arrival at Coqualeetza in 1915:

> We arrived in Chilliwack (from Yale) in early
> September 1915. We got off the CN Train and
> there was no transportation between
> Chilliwack and Sardis. So my mother, my five-
> year-old brother, and I walked. My mother told
> us not to cry. My brother was so little that he
> had to live on the girls' side of the school so the
> big girls could take care of him.

A teacher gave them each a number to memorize to be used as their permanent identification. They were put in charge of a girl named Mabel (whose mother also attended All Hallows) and taken to the enormous dining hall for supper — boys on one side, girls on the other. Proper dining manners were strictly followed at the table while a staff member slowly paced up and down the centre aisle.

Shortly after the supper hour, it was time to prepare for bed. Hope's bed was in a small attic room with three other girls. She sorted her belongings and listened to the matron recite the nighttime regimen. She couldn't sleep, worrying about little Henry. At 6:00 a.m., the matron called each girl's name and they were expected to quickly wash and go to the dining hall to listen to a talk and blessing by Principal Raley before eating breakfast.

For students coming from reserves, it was a devastating transition to move from an easy-going, affectionate family environment into a cold institution with severe rules and restrictions. Many could not understand or speak English; others would try to translate. Hope realized it was an advantage to be English-speaking, accustomed to English ways and English food, but she was nonetheless desperately frightened and homesick. Sophie had always demanded proper behaviour and manners from her children but had a much softer demeanour than the teachers at Coqualeetza.

Children arriving at the school would be washed down thoroughly with Lifebuoy soap and their heads examined for lice. If lice were found, their head would be disinfected and they would receive a short, blunt haircut. Lice inspections were frequent and some of the children later nicknamed the lice: *meatsils*.

Hope recalled:

> We found it difficult following the day-to-day routine. We were up so early and went to school for half a day and worked for half a day. I had gone to school in Yale for one year so I had my grade one and they put me in the primary grades. It was a tent with one board wall.

Letters home were allowed only every six weeks and were censored by a staff member. Family visits, including siblings of the opposite sex living in the school, were also allowed only every six weeks. The times when Hope was able to visit Henry, she could see the desperation on his face. She knew the boys were treated more harshly than the girls but she was completely powerless to help him. She could only hope that things would improve with time.

Henry Castle, age 5

Henry was moved into the boys' dormitory after a few months of being babied in the girls' dormitory. The older girls had the job of caring for and comforting the very young children arriving at the school and they became accustomed to the distressing sounds of children sobbing and crying, especially in bed at night.

Henry was smaller than others his age and was particularly terrified of older boys. One boy took great pleasure in teasing and bullying him, constantly saying, "*You're* not an Indian." He didn't know how to cope with them or how to respond to the strange, acerbic manner of the English teachers. But he was extremely fast on his feet and eventually learned to sense when to quickly escape a bullying situation. The times when he couldn't get away, he just took the punishment and put on a stern face. It became routine. Being sent to Coqualeetza and the harsh treatment he received was so agonizingly shattering to Henry that he forever kept silent about his life at Coqualeetza.

When their first summer holidays arrived, Hope and Henry were sent to the Coqualeetza summer camp for students who did not go home for the summer holidays. It was usually at Crescent Beach or at times in White Rock, supervised by at least three staff members. One staff member commented that "it is the health resort and building-up place for the native boy and girl and especially those not too robust a build." A staff member's report on the summer camp was written in a school annual:

> The Camp lasted a month and was truly a tent
> life. The swimming in the salt water, the
> gathering of shell fish, the boating, the evening
> camp fires, the sing-song and marshmallow
> toasts, the Tuck Shop, [*a food shop used by Indian*
> *boarding schools, clubs and campsites*] morning
> and evening Prayers, the Sunday Service in the
> open air, were all most enjoyable. We have

heard that Daily Inspection was "the fly in the ointment" but even a camp must be properly run.

There were various reasons why many students could not go home for the summer — the main reason being the distances to travel to their village homes. It was economically impossible. On many reserves, parents were working in canneries full time. Also, some students were orphans.

One of the many important visitors to Coqualeetza, and a friend to Principal Raley, was Mr. David Spencer of Spencer's Department Stores. He owned property in the Chilliwack area and often visited the school. He was interested in Indian art and history and later displayed pieces from the Raley Collection in his Vancouver department store. It was said that when Hope and Henry first arrived at Coqualeetza he enquired about adopting them, believing they were orphans.

After the painful event of leaving her children at Coqualeetza, Sophie was determined to carry out her plan to live with Joseph in Vancouver. She eventually purchased the train fare, packed up little Ruth, and bravely travelled to Vancouver, resolving never to return to Yale again.

When they arrived, she found her way from the terminal to Joseph's east end apartment and waited for him to arrive home. She and Joseph had acquired a great fondness for each other and she knew she could count on his kindness and generosity. Just as she had envisioned, he graciously welcomed them in to his home. It was said that he hardly recognized her when she arrived; she had become so ill and thin.

Joseph Andrews
On the job as a longshoreman
(date unknown)

Joseph earned a fair wage as a longshoreman foreman and they soon were able to move to a modest house on Semlin Drive in the east end. Sophie felt so safe and secure with Joseph that she began calling herself, Mrs. Andrews.

In just over a year, they were expecting their first child. On February 20, 1917, a boy, William Fredrick Andrews, was born.

The year of William's birth was the same year as Hope and Henry's first summer holiday in Vancouver. Sophie had managed to make only one trip to Sardis to visit them during their first school year. They could hardly contain their excitement when they arrived at the station in Vancouver and saw Sophie, Ruth and little William waiting to greet them at the station.

That summer was a memorable time in Hope's young life — she bought her first *real* bathing suit with her own money, in stylish black cotton. Although she was only nine years old, the next-door neighbour had offered her a job as a daytime babysitter, paying twenty-five cents a day, with the provision that she cooks lunch for the children. The only lunch she actually knew how to cook was a hard-boiled egg and toast, which she proudly served every day. (The young girls were not taught to cook at Coqualeetza.)

Being the motherly older sister to her siblings and taking care of baby William, Hope sometimes felt lumbered with babysitting but was grateful just to have a break from Coqualeetza. She accepted Joseph in her life, with some apprehension, but was soon referring to him as Pop.

Henry was not so easily accepting of Joseph, or of going back to Coqualeetza. He pleaded with Sophie to let him stay home, but Sophie was firm in her decision that he must go back. Henry felt only a life of punishment at school. Being sent back after the summer holidays could probably be described similarly to another residential school student's memory, written in the book, *Resistance and Renewal*, by Celia Haig-Brown. A student described going back to residential school after the summer holidays:

> I knew I couldn't stay home. I knew that. But
> the times that really, really gets to the bottom
> of my soul: the first day back...you wake up in
> the morning and you see this white ceiling. You
> may as well have a knife and stab me through
> my heart.

Hope and Henry took little Ruth back to Coqualeetza with them in September. Sophie had told Ruth many times what a great privilege it was to go to such a fine school and Ruth was ready and anxious to go. It was an exciting adventure for her to ride on the train to

Ruth Castle, age 5

Chilliwack and she felt perfectly safe to be going anywhere with her brother and much-loved and ad-mired sister, who she now called Hopie.

Ruth began kindergarten around the same time as her fifth birthday, September 6, 1917. She loved the idea of going to Coqualeetza but of course would not know then that the school would be her home for the next sixteen years. Growing up in a family home would never be in the Castle children's future. She would hardly remember August Castle and would always think of Joseph as their 'Pop'.

Ruth tried hard to do what was expected of her and flourished in her schoolwork. Principal Raley was always concerned with the adjustment of all the young kindergarten children arriving at Coqualeetza and he devoted much attention to Ruth, watching over and encouraging her.

Coqualeetza students and staff, c. 1918

~oo0oo~

Chapter Six:
A Unique Reverend

Dr. Raley on Vancouver Street holding an
Indian basket (date unknown)

Originally from England, Reverend Raley worked with native Indians of British Columbia for 35 years. He made a thorough study of the Indian language in Kitimat and was given a number of Indian names during his residence there. One he greatly prized was Abskamala, given to him by the chief of the village. It means, "the raven that fed the hungry people." The Reverend and his helpers had travelled for five miles by canoe to answer smoke signals of distress by some stranded Kitslass Indians.

During a radio broadcast of the Coqualeetza choir, Reverend Raley spoke of the history of British Columbia's Indians and the philosophy of the totem. (One of his many published books is entitled, *Our Totem Poles – A Souvenir of British Columbia*.)

Following is an extract from this radio broadcast:

> You have been listening to the choir of the Coqualeetza Indian Residential School of Sardis. This choir is made up from the nationalities which form the Native people of British Columbia. They come from all parts and represent the Hiadah-Tsimpsheam, Kwaguilth, and Salish Nations, speaking four distinct languages as well as English.
>
> They have been here since before the time of Christ, two thousand years at least, and

possessed the country in its entirety until the white man came. The people lived a primitive life in a vast country, close to nature's heart, in the great out-of-doors, unrestrained by the white man, or the white man's laws.

By rigid training and abstemious living, they became a people of great physical endurance. They were free to camp and roam …. hunt and fish, within their own tribal territory at the time without restraint. There were no game laws and no Fisheries Act.

Their social life in the winter was spent in airy tribal or communal houses where they were free to enjoy the primitive ceremonies, feasts and gatherings according to rules and regulations which they punctiliously observed.

A code of ethics and morals was adhered to, suitable to his environment, inherited tendencies, his natural culture, his feelings and traditions.

His religion was polytheistic, endowing all things of the material world animate or inanimate with spirit force and form. This is the foundation of his totemism, which affected the whole of his life from birth to death. All the social, economic, cultural and religious life of the Native tribes of British Columbia was built on the totemic system. The sun was his earliest totem and children were taught to speak with respect and reverence. They were taught:

> The sun is your father
> The sky his abode
> Growth is his daily concern
> Beware least you spoil his work
> Or mar the beauty of his creation.

When the Reverend arrived at Coqualeetza in 1914, he found the school in appalling, filthy conditions. With his exceptional command of the English language and remarkable persuasive powers, he was able to convince the Department of Indian Affairs to provide additional per capita grants for school improvements and increased subsidies from the Methodist Church missionary societies. In his attempt to counter the unnatural effects of institutionalization on children and provide a bit of the home spirit, he requested two small cottages, one for small boys and one for small girls, stating:

> It is essential the younger children should have more motherly care. These qualities - love for home and respect for society alone will inspire children as they grow up with the desires to preserve the nation. Without these qualities, there will be no, or little, desire either for true citizenship or patriotic life of the Nation.

His charm and knowledge enabled him to acquire the connections and respect from officials of authority that he needed to obtain improvements. With his persuasion and, at times, flattery, he was able to have the old school rendered inadequate and obtain the funds to build a new school. In a reference to Dr. Duncan C. Scott, Superintendent of Indian Affairs, Reverend Raley wrote:

> Dr. Scott has given innumerable evidences of
> his ability fairly and justly to look after Canada's
> wards. His kindly spirit and natural dignity
> never failed to impress the Indian people.
> There is no space here to enumerate my claim
> that Dr. Scott is the most influential and best
> friend the Indians ever had. His policy has been
> one of progressive advancement.

Working with Dr. Scott and others, they received the approval from the dominion government to finance the cost of the new building, which was said to have cost $200,000.00, and accommodated approximately 220 students.

Reverend Raley was referred to as Dr. Raley, after being honoured with a Doctor of Divinity Degree by Union College for humanitarian work among B.C. Indians.

A study entitled, *A New Understanding of Things Indian, George Raley's Negotiation of the Residential*

School Experience, by Paige Raibmon, was published in a B.C. Studies report of 1993. Following are several extracts:

George H. Raley arrived from England with a keen interest in Native culture, feeling that "in order to understand the attitude of the Indian towards Christianity and white civilization it was necessary to study the ethnological background of the people." Raley's philosophy both departed from and converged with prevailing thought. "Instead of educators attempting to eradicate all vestiges of Indian culture, they ought to attempt to develop it and build on it rather than crush out all that is Indian."

Raley took his position as principal of a residential school for Native children seriously and felt a deep sense of responsibility towards the students in his charge. He described himself as standing *in loco parentis* to the students at Coqualeetza, and he insisted that "this parental relation is not a mere legal form; it is an actual and concrete responsibility." In Raley, this sense of responsibility included an unusual sensitivity towards Native culture and values. In his speeches and writings, Raley emphasized the positive educational and moral structures of Native society:

If we think the Indians of B.C. had no form of education we have another guess coming. True they had no school houses, text books and other appurtenances necessary to education today. But they had that creative urge to grow, to make, to progress, to develop, an intuition without which there can be no education. Indians of both sexes were taught to be clean, truthful, honest, generous, hospitable and brave. Now a race which inculcates such sound virtues in the minds of their children can hardly be called depraved or debased.

Although Raley was never able to implement a full cottage system at Coqualeetza, he was successful at infusing the school with *a bit of the home spirit* and, thus, at mitigating some of the negative aspects of the congregate system. Raley lessened the institutional atmosphere in many other ways, ranging from festivities on special occasions to rides around the schoolyard in his car. These efforts tempered the harmful disruption of social bonds and created an enjoyable environment for the children. Bonds that formed the basis of life-long relationships were created among students as well as between students and staff.

Raley would have been a more typical missionary had he remained strictly within the framework of Victorian attitudes towards Aboriginal people. His interest in Native culture and his various programs and proposals were part of an emerging discourse surrounding Native issues. Raley himself can be considered a site where traditional Victorian values met nascent cultural ideologies – where reverend met anthropologist.

Principal Raley visiting summer
camp (date unknown)

Dr. Raley had a highly developed sense of museum purpose and chose to have his treasured collection remain in B.C. where it might be seen and enjoyed by collectors and the general public alike. His collection formed an important nucleus of the Northwest Coast Collections in the new University of British Columbia's Museum of Anthropology in 1948. It consisted of 800 pieces and contained objects from the entire British Columbia coast, from Tshimpshian in the north to the Salish in the south. Today, much of this collection is shown in the Haisla section of the museum. He used his collection of Indian folklore and legendary tales for periodic lectures to the students. A former student later commented that he appreciated these lectures, learning about other tribes in British Columbia, their habits and culture, which he would not otherwise have learned in another residential or public school.

Following is an excerpt from an article printed in The Vancouver Province, of February 1957:

The first justice of the peace, judge, postmaster, doctor, meteorologist and minister in the wilderness of Kitimat will celebrate his 94th birthday on Valentine's Day.

Rev. George H. Raley, D.D., B.C.'s pioneer missionary, will delay the celebrations until next Monday when he will entertain about 110 friends at his home.

Dr. Raley retired in 1934 after serving as principal of Coqualeetza Indian school at Sardis from 1914. "And he hasn't missed having a party since 1935," says [his daughter] Mrs. Charlton.

Dr. Raley, with his wife, the only white woman for miles, established the first mission at Kitimat Indian village. He ministered to the needs of the [Kitimat] Indian people for 13 years. He published the north coast's first newspaper in 1896, turning it out with a hand press.

He still belongs to the B.C. Historical Society, is honorary president of the B.C. Historical and Scientific Association, and belongs to the Canadian Authors' Association. Dr. Raley holds fellowships in the Royal Geographical Society and the Society of Arts.

At ninety years of age he regularly visited Indian patients in Vancouver hospitals. He often renewed acquaintances with those who were his pupils or who were his parishioners in coastal villages.

At one time fifty percent of the Village Council at Skidegate on the Queen Charlotte Islands graduated from Coqualeetza.

Dr. Raley died in 1959 at the age of 96.

~oo0oo~

Chapter Seven:
'Shun not the Struggle'

Coqualeetza Staff and Monitors, 1924

Hopie's self-confidence grew through her primary school years. She enjoyed piano lessons and was elected to perform a piano solo at a school concert. She chose to play her favourite song, Largo. Everyone told her she played it beautifully, with no mistakes.

Hopie had always received high grades and was anxiously looking forward to moving up to the junior grades. Then she received some stunning news that completely shattered her. With no reasonable explanation, she was told she could not move up, she was too small. (Because of staff shortages, half-work days, and the emphasis for girls on household work, it was common for girls at that time to drift along in the same grade for two or three years.)

She later recalled:

> When I was fifteen, they put me from the
> primary grades right up to grade eight. When it
> came time to write the exams, I was so nervous
> I was sick to my stomach and couldn't finish
> writing the exams so had to write them over
> again the next year. I passed the second time I
> wrote the exams.

The Vancouver Sun newspaper once quoted a 1920s Coqualeetza teacher as saying:

> They are not as clever as white children, but
> they try to get on ever so much harder, and

considering they have not the benefit of hereditary training along educational lines, they do remarkably well. The girls do six weeks in the kitchen, cooking, and six weeks in the sewing room, learning how to sew, knit, crochet, darn and generally make themselves useful.

Culinary Arts was Hopie's least favourite course. The towering piles of plates to wash were overwhelming. "This job will go to others after your turn," the teacher, Miss Bailey, would often remind them for encouragement.

Miss Bailey wrote the following report in a school annual.

CULINARY DEPARTMENT

Theory: 2 hours. Application: 18 hours weekly.

Make miles of bread; cook dozens of cattle and boatloads of fish.

Do dishes.

Report by Miss Bailey, Culinary Department:

Another busy year has rolled away for this Department with all its hundreds of puddings, pies, cakes and toothsome viands. Besides the tons of vegetables, meats and fish which have to be prepared through-out the year, tons of fruit are prepared for canning along with the

> making of hundreds of pounds of marmalades,
> jams, jellies and pickles. The girls do this work
> cheerfully.

Health, nutrition and bacteria became an obsession for Hopie. She read and re-read every book she could find on these subjects, especially anything to do with germs. She became such an expert on the subject that she entered a province-wide contest on health and nutrition and ranked third in the province. She had a life-long habit of whisking away dirty dishes and food from the table, sometimes before the meal was finished.

The school clothes — ugly boots, bloomers and heavy leggings were a standard part of dress in residential schools. One student maintained that the big boots were to help prevent the kids from running away. It was not compulsory to wear school uniforms at Coqualeetza if they had other appropriate clothing to wear. The senior girls made their own dresses in sewing class and they all made their own graduation dresses. But most of the work in sewing class, according to Hopie, was "patching the dreaded heavy work clothes."

Although Hopie would never dare to rebel against authority, she had a slightly mischievous nature. Her daughter, Doreen, wrote the following tale:

The Parcel

Sophie sent a parcel of clothing to her three kids at school, Hope, Henry and Ruth Castle. Because Hope was the oldest, the parcel was sent to her. This was just too much for her. She had never seen so many new clothes in her entire life! She gave in to the temptation - she kept them all. Her own stuff, Henry's running shoes and Ruth's dress that was too small. She wore them with pride and, no doubt, some guilt.

Hopie abided by all the religious and moral teachings at Coqualeetza. The unrelenting discipline of the school contributed to her self-imposed high standard of behaviour at all times. Being the oldest child, she felt a deep responsibility for Henry and Ruth, giving her quite a serious outlook during her childhood.

Hope Castle, approx. 13 years old

She remembered, and took seriously, Dr. Raley's words...

> The highest aim is to make Christian citizens of
> the pupils, and so they are taught to *Fear God*
> and *Honour the King*. We seek to give the girls
> a clear idea of what true womanhood means.
> This embraces a study of the virtues and graces,
> which go to make happy homes. For the boys
> we crave a conception of true manliness, a love

for honest labour and an intelligent interest in the affairs of the state.

In all, we seek to instil a reverence for sacred things and respect for the rights of others. We have visions of leadership for some and a healthy atmosphere of usefulness for many, and the following lines seem to express what we desire all shall learn:

> We are not here to play, to dream, to drift,
> We have hard work to do, and loads to lift,
> Shun not the struggle, face it,
> 'tis God's gift.
> Be strong, be strong!

Hopie was proud that her name was listed near the top few of her class in her junior high graduation year. She confidently played the piano piece, La Cinquantaine, at the graduation ceremony.

The histories of each student was printed in the annual. Hopie's read:

Tribe:	Salish
Chief Occupation:	Talking and giggling
Aversion:	Patching stiff overalls
Ambition:	To be a nurse
Pet Expression:	Oh, that's gorgeous!

Graduating Class, 1924
(Hope is circled)

Soon after the graduation ceremonies, the old school was demolished and the children moved into their newly-built school. Hopie did not experience living in the new school with Henry and Ruth. She packed her belongings, said a tearful goodbye to the staff and all her friends, and anxiously boarded the train at the Chilliwack station. Destination: the *gorgeous* city of Vancouver. She had planned for this day for as long as she could remember.

Hope Castle, age 17, 1924

A morbid event happened to Henry when he was about ten years old. It was an incident that Sophie never revealed to other family members but was forever embedded in Henry's memory. Hopie and Ruth knew, because it happened at Coqualeetza. This is the story:

Sophie received an urgent message from the Coqualeetza matron stating that Henry had been stricken with a severe case of double pneumonia and had died. Hearing this unbelievably stunning news, all Sophie could do was to instruct the matron to have his body packed in a crate and shipped by rail to Vancouver.

While waiting for the arrival of the crate, she tried to prepare herself for the gruesome task of opening the box. When she finally struck up the nerve to open it, she was astounded at what she saw. She lifted back the corner of the blanket and saw his face – it was as white as a sheet and his eyes were slightly open. She then discovered he was barely breathing. Panic stricken, she somehow managed to get him to the hospital, praying he would survive. Miraculously, he did.

After a short time in the hospital, Henry was nursed back to health and was soon strong enough to be sent back to Coqualeetza.

Henry was not able to keep his bitterness hidden. He believed nobody hated Coqualeetza more than he did and he held a standing grudge towards each and every

Coqualeetza monitor. When older students became monitors (mainly for the purpose of helping the teachers' workloads), they had a hierarchy that could be threatening and some used this power for cruel intimidation. He maintained that when he left school, he never wanted anything more to do with Indians and nobody was to even mention the word, *Coqualeetza*. In later years, he said that when he had tried to run away from the school, he was punished by a male teacher who had hanged him by his thumbs.

When Henry became old enough to take care of the animals, he began to enjoy the farm duties. He looked forward to brushing and harnessing the horses every morning, preparing them for their day's work. He acquired a great love for animals and his life at school greatly improved. An ex-student recalled: "When Henry had the job of feeding the pigs, he taught them to say grace. He trained them to always grunt before being fed. They had better manners than us."

Ultimately, Henry developed an extraordinary, often mischievous, sense of humour and his eyes had a perpetual, impish sparkle. He was quite proud of the time he placed a frog in a young, female teacher's desk, and boasted: "When she opened the drawer and it jumped out, she shrieked and leaped onto her chair. It was the first time I had ever seen a woman's knees!"

Working on Coqualeetza farm (date unknown)

Antagonizing Hopie and Ruth was great fun for Henry. The girls were not amused one summer when they found he had secretly replaced all their flower seeds with potatoes. The girls would often retaliate by speaking to each other in a slow and exaggerated Indian accent. He would plug his ears and shout, "Stop talking like an Indian!" When the children occasionally had the treat of an ice cream cone, Henry knew how to get Hopie's cone for himself. He would put his face right up to the cone and breathe on it. She would then stretch out her arm and hand it to him with total disdain. He also enjoyed teaching his brother William (Bill) some of his ideas to torment the girls. They once held Hopie to the floor and cut off all her beautifully manicured fingernails.

Henry in school uniform, approx. 12 years old

During his school years, Henry occasionally travelled to Yale to visit August and would go along with him on some of his exciting adventures. This is when Henry began his keen interest in exploring and rock hunting. Sophie had not passed her bitterness for August on to her children and they were not cognizant of the entire 'August Castle situation'. Henry was impressed with his father and deeply admired him.

At this time, during the early1920s, Sophie sometimes sent young Bill to Yale to stay with his grandmother Ellen (Joseph's mother) for part of the summer so that there would be room for the Castle children when they came home to Vancouver. (Ellen moved to Yale after the death of her husband, Joseph Comeyne.) It was said that Ellen was psychic and would advise August on prospecting sites to explore. Bill recalled seeing August, who was approximately sixty years old at that time and in excellent physical condition, outrunning and catching some teenagers who had tipped over several outhouses.

Henry's self-esteem rose when he became a valued member of the Coqualeetza track team. He had done well in the trades of shoemaking, blacksmithing, mechanical engineering, carpentry, and baking. At one point, the carpentry class built an entire three-car garage, which included a concrete floor and electric wiring. These courses would be particularly useful to him later in life.

Coqualeetza was Henry's home until he was nineteen years old. He worked in the Coqualeetza bakery for a year to earn enough money to start his independence. He was eager to go out in the world. Unfortunately, he had one important drawback — he had trouble reading and he could not write. He would never reveal, and it was never known, just how difficult this was for him. But the strong will and courage that had developed from his miserable school days would never allow him to be put down or bullied again. His Indian name given to him was The Fox.

Surprisingly, unlike most other Coqualeetza students, Henry did not leave school with a high opinion of Dr. Raley. His bitterness was against everybody connected to Coqualeetza. He told his brother Bill that the sound of train whistles forever caused a knot in his stomach — a reminder of "the train back to hell."

Henry Castle, 1927

~oo0oo~

Chapter Eight:
Vestigia Nulla Retrorsum
- No Backward Step

Student body at front entrance
Coqualeetza Residential School, 1928

After the performance of Princess Chrysanthemum, the last operetta in the old school, the students moved into their new school, renamed Coqualeetza Residential School. They were thrilled and amazed to see and experience all the new, modern conveniences. They were especially excited when they learned that there would be moving pictures shown bi-weekly in the new auditorium. The school had three times the floor area of the old building and was the most modern building erected in Canada for the education of Indian children at that time. (The bricks from the demolished building were re-used in the construction of the Canadian Legion building on Main Street in Chilliwack.)

The students were proud of their new school motto, **Vestigia Nulla Retrorsum — No Backward Step,** engraved in huge black and gold letters over the front entrance of the school. The following photo shows the new Coqualeetza building protruding from behind the old building.

Coqualeetza Industrial Institute

Coqualeetza Residential School

Aerial View of Coqueleetza Residential School

Because of its fine reputation, Coqualeetza attracted many important visitors who were often asked to participate in a tree-planting ceremony on the school's beautiful, lush grounds.

Visit from His Honour Randolph Bruce, Lieutenant-Governor of British Columbia, 1928 (Coqualeetza Cadets standing in back)

Every occasion was performed with great pomp and ceremony and guests were usually entertained at a formal luncheon with Dr. and Mrs. Raley at the principal's residence. Although this house was off-limits to the students, the household manager often gave instructions on fine English dining to a few chosen older girls. The students later called this house The Big House.

Principal's residence – built on the Coqualeetza grounds in 1910.
This house was said to be one of the finest homes in Sardis.

This Victorian-style sitting room, illustrated in the 1924
commencement annual, was Dr. Raley's definition of
"a bit of the home spirit."

Dr. Raley succeeded to incorporate further training that he believed would help the students' independence when leaving the school. By the 1930s, in addition to the academic training, all the following were in full force:

Agriculture and Horticulture
Auto Mechanics
Blacksmithing
Boat Building
Boy Scouts and Girl Guides
Brownies and Wolf Cubs
C.G.I.T.
Cadets
Carpentry & Mechanical Training
Choir
Indian Handicrafts

Indian Pageants
Manufacturing shirts & dresses
Manual Training
Musical Training and Recitals
   (violin and piano)
Nursing
Printing Department
School Orchestra
Sewing and other handiwork
St. John's Ambulance course
Student Council

Coqualeetza - Main Entrance

Nursing Class

Boat Building

Indian Crafts

Girls and boys basketball teams, girls softball team,
Olympiad trophies won that year and boys football tea, 1931

The most unique aspect of Dr. Raley's curriculum was to attempt to sustain a native Indian cultural presence. He covered the main hall and reception room walls of the new school with his collection of Indian art so the students could appreciate and be proud of their art and heritage.

The Music Department increasingly advanced pupils to their ability. Throughout the year, the pupils in this department brightened social functions and lecture evenings with musical selections. Many pupils studied for examinations of the Associated Board of the Royal Academy of Music and The Royal College of Music. Some finished their Toronto Conservatory examinations.

Sports were of high importance at Coqualeetza and generated great school spirit, which was not highly approved by the Department of Indian Affairs. There were fine soccer, basketball, baseball, and track teams that participated in the annual Sports Day activities. When it was cold enough in the winter, they prepared an outdoor ice rink for the boys to play hockey. In 1931, the first annual Indian School Olympiad in Canada was held at Coqualeetza.

Since Coqualeetza's curriculum ended at the completion of grade nine, Dr. Raley acquired enough funding to allow qualified and willing students to room and board at Coqualeetza and continue on to the public high school in Chilliwack. In other residential schools, Indian agents denied students the right to attend high school.

Dr. Raley retired as principal of Coqualeetza in 1934 and was replaced by Capt. R. C. Scott, of the British Columbia Marine Mission of The United Church of Canada.

~oo0oo~

Chapter Nine:
The Last Farewell

Coqualeetza Campus (rear), 1931

Ruth was as happy as could be at Coqualeetza. She was an honour student and participated in everything she possibly could — piano lessons, track and field, operettas, C.G.I.T. (Canadian Girls in Training), Girl Guides, and the Student Council.

Ruth   Princess Chrysanthemum Operetta, 1924

Relationships of the opposite sex were positively not allowed at Coqualeetza and there would be dire consequences if anyone dared to consider such a thing. However, an attraction began between Ruth and Oliver Adams (nicknamed Skinny) when they were in their early teens. It was undeniably first love for both of them and everyone in the school was aware of it. They managed to see each other only at assemblies and sports activities, and perhaps at summer camp. Occasionally a few of the more audacious boys, including Skinny, would find ways to sneak over to the girls' side, but it was an extremely risky thing to do. (Oliver Adams was a top student and athlete and was voted 'the most popular boy' one year.)

Oliver (Skinny) Adams

Ruth Castle with Trosky
(Mrs. Raley's dog)

There was hardly a mention of sex at Coqualeetza. The school nurse, Miss Dale, a young spinster and missionary, made the only feeble attempt. She would teach the girls about the body in nursing class but would only go so far. "If you have a cold sore it means you've had sex," she warned. After that, anyone with a cold sore was immediately suspect, but the girls were still not clear on what this meant. It was very confusing.

Miss Dale's Nursing Class   Miss
Dale   Ruth

Delavina 'Dolly' Allard was Ruth's best friend at school. Everything was enormously fun to them. Both were bouncy, enthusiastic, and quite competitive. They were alike in many ways, and Dolly also had a boyfriend, named Percy Gladstone. There was a common saying among the girls, one that Ruth and Dolly often said to each other when one resented the other for obtaining a higher achievement. They would say, slowly, in a low, huffy, voice, "Think you're bigger than Martha." Martha was not big and most didn't know who she was or how she got involved in these competitions, but the saying was perfectly understood by all the girls.

When guest speakers, such as university professors, visited the school to lecture, the students were instructed to try to look intelligent and to ask intelligent questions. This was not always easy to do, especially when hearing a talk on male and female trees. Some examples of lectures were:

Elizabethan Song Composers

The Psychology of Totemism

The Oriental Problem and the Solution of it

Booker T. Washington of Tuskegee (assisted by cornet solos)

The General Breeds and Care of Live Stock

How We Got Our English Bible

Have Plants Morals?

The students did not go home for Christmas, but Ruth remembered the season at Coqualeetza with great fondness. She later wrote: "And Christmas, how the school was transformed into a fairyland with cedar festoons and holly decorating the halls and the giant Christmas trees with a present for every boy and girl, no child was forgotten. Those indeed were the most wonderful Christmases."

The 1930 school annual listed the description of Coqualeetza's Christmas dinner.

If anyone doubts there was feasting and merrymaking at Coqualeetza at Christmas, let him read the Christmas Day Menu:

Breakfast: Corn Flakes and Milk, Parker House
Rolls with Honey, Cocoa;

Dinner: Roast Goose, Dressing and Gravy,
Mashed Potatoes, Stewed Tomatoes,
Cucumber Pickles, Apple Sauce, Plum Pudding,
Caramel Sauce, Lemonade, Christmas Cake,
Fruit, Candy, and Nuts;

Supper: Mince Meat Turnovers, Sugar Cookies,
Marble Cake, Jelly and Custard, Raisin Bread
and Butter, Christmas Cake, Coffee. There!

Church services and prayers were customary at
Coqualeetza and Ruth was a true believer. Religion was a
serious part of her life. When she first heard the story of
Jesus being nailed to the cross, it deeply affected her. She
remembered crying and agonizing over it for days and
couldn't pull herself out of bed. Her religious teachings
were obvious in her valedictorian address for the 1931
Coqualeetza graduation. (*Elfinland* refers to their last
Christmas Operetta, The Stolen Princess.)

Our school has been like 'Elfinland,' joyous,
happy. 'Graduateland' too, is interesting. As
we look through a mystery window, we glimpse
'knowledge and success' standing quite aloof,
while opportunity knocks at the door. Over the
cliff, sin and temptation smile winningly. We
wonder, do we fall?

Experience gives a squeal of delight for he is eager to introduce us to his friend, 'Life.' A birdie, 'Courage,' sings cheerfully near by. But hope comes gently to greet us. As she takes us to the Alpine Path, we joyfully recognize two beautiful stars. They are, *I live for the good that I can do* and *No backward step.*

We've had lovely and happy hours at Elfinland. The memory of our schoolmates, teachers and Principal will always inspire us. We sense a deep gratitude and will try to live worthily, for we take with us the high ideals and beautiful traditions of our school. We wish the Principal and Staff every success and hope all their ambitions for us will be realized.

We will have to choose the friends of our later life. Perhaps wisdom will not always guide us, but we realize there is One whom we can trust. One who will share our troubles and joys alike, whom we can always love and who will always love us; our truest friend — God.

-- Ruth Castle, Valedictorian

Graduating Class, 1931   Dolly   Ruth

   Most of the students had nicknames, or 'class names.'
In Ruth's graduating class there were some unique class
names, such as: Dreams, Picky, Mush Junior, Shordy,
Fig, Marigold, Cheaky, Dolly, Birdie, Beans and Tuffy. A
student from another class, Susan, was known as 'Nigger
Susie' because of her dark skin.   The students were
completely unaware of the harmful effect of this word.
Racist words were widely used during that time period,
and for decades to come.

   Some of the students knew of the difficulties they
would likely face when they returned home to reserves or
ventured out into the working world.   Many students
seldom or never went home for the summer and would be

like strangers to their families and communities, losing much or all of their own language, their culture, or knowing a family life. They had worked and studied hard to be accepted as 'citizens' of Canada.

Ruth and Hopie routinely corresponded by mail. In Ruth's letters to Hopie, she often mentioned how excited she was to go to Chilliwack High and how she *wished* she had a winter coat to wear. Hopie soon sent her enough money from her meagre savings to buy a new coat. During the Depression years, it wouldn't have occurred to Ruth to mention this need to Sophie.

The years at Chilliwack High School were fond memories for Ruth. The students would walk, ride bikes or take a bus to school and be back at Coqualeetza immediately after school. The more casual atmosphere at a public school and making new friends was an enjoyable experience for her. She also obtained a business degree and worked as secretary to Dr. Raley after graduating from Chilliwack High. Ruth adored Dr. Raley and considered him to be the most caring and intelligent human being she had ever known. He was her father figure.

Ruth was twenty-one years old when she left Coqualeetza. She had lived at the school since she was five years old and thought of Coqualeetza as her home. Most of her classmates were like family to her, and Dr.

and Mrs. Raley, Miss Bailey and Miss Adams had been like her own parents. Saying goodbye was extremely emotional for her.

Oliver and Ruth did not continue their relationship after they left school. They would not see each other again for many years.

Ruth Castle, age 21, 1933

During the late 1930s, several students contracted tuberculosis and were treated in one of the school buildings, known as The Preventorium. As more and more children were infected with the disease, Coqualeetza became a T.B. hospital and Coqualeetza Residential School officially closed in 1941. Many people were outraged at this decision and believed a hospital could have been built elsewhere.

Years later, Ruth made a tribute to Dr. Raley, stating:

> I feel that much of the good influence of Coqualeetza was due to the unique thinking of Dr. Raley. He emphasized over and over the need for higher education. Dr. Raley was able to get the funding and urged pupils to get as much education as possible. We understand that, for this reason, Coqualeetza was not popular with the District of Indian Affairs. The DIA pushed to close the school down and finally were successful in turning it into a T.B. hospital for the Indian people.

There are many differing opinions of Coqualeetza Residential School. The following paragraph is an extract from the "Coqualeetza, Legacies of Land Use" in the book *A Stó:lō-Coast Salish Historical Atlas.*

> Like its predecessor, the new school promoted a particular brand of education for Aboriginal

people. The school focused on farm and industrial work for boys and domestic work for girls, at the expense of academic subjects. Nonetheless, many Stó:lō thought Coqualeetza offered students a better education than other residential schools. In fact, to the chagrin of priests and despite their own religious affiliations, some Roman Catholic Stó:lō parents, especially those from the nearby reserves, preferred to enrol their children at Coqualeetza rather than at St. Mary's Catholic school, across the river in Mission City. This said, Coqualeetza still operated within a colonial plan designed to assimilate Aboriginal children into Xwelitm [white] culture by separating them from their families and traditions and by punishing them for speaking their own languages

~oo0oo~

Part Two

Chapter Ten:
Life in Vancouver

Sophie and Hopie walking on Granville Street, 1925

After the birth of William in 1917, there were four more Andrews children, all daughters: Kathleen (Tootsie) in 1919; Doris (Dodie) in 1921; Isabel in 1925; and Frances (Frankie) in 1929. Joseph continued to earn a good, steady income and they moved from the small house on Semlin Drive to a larger house on Pandora Street in Vancouver's east end.

William Andrews, 1918

Sophie on left holding Tootsie;
William in front on stairs.
Visiting a friend in North Vancouver.

Sophie kept her children immaculately clean but was not terribly strict with them. The house was always comfortable with a warm atmosphere. Her starched, ruffled curtains covered each window, her fine embroidery and crochet work was placed on all the appropriate places, and the sound of her well-worn, classical gramophone records constantly filled the air.

Hopie happily settled into the Andrews house in the summer of 1924 and registered in the local high school, Britannia High. Although she was tentative about attending a public school, it was not nearly as challenging as she thought it might be. Her quiet, gentle manner enabled her to fit in easily and she loved everything about the school. To earn her room and board, she took several housekeeping jobs in the evenings and on weekends. She often boasted that her employers were impressed with her exemplary domestic training.

She soon had a busy social life and even began dating the occasional young gentleman. According to her younger sister, Dodie, she spent hours chatting to her friends on the telephone and preparing for various social events. Dodie recalled being fascinated watching her roll her stockings down to her knees like the trendy *roll'em girls*. Sophie often had a slight bite to her teasing and would sometimes say, "You better watch out, your sister Ruth might come and steal your boyfriends away."

Hope Castle, age 19

Hopie and friends

During her final year at Britannia High, Hopie registered in a nanny-training course. When her course was completed, she was offered the perfect job opportunity — a live-in nanny position for a wealthy family in Vancouver's west end. The home was in her favourite area of Vancouver — three blocks from English Bay. She felt privileged to live in such a luxurious home and especially enjoyed being able to dash to the beach for a swim. She usually went home on her days off, especially since Henry moved in from Coqualeetza. She said there was never a dull moment when Henry was around.

Then, after several years of various nanny jobs, she became daringly adventurous. She began pondering the idea of moving on to a different type of job, one that would give her more freedom. In 1929, she packed up her bags and moved to the small, coastal town of Bella Bella, B.C. to work in the fish cannery. She had no idea how long she would stay, but told Sophie it was definitely a temporary move. Several of her girlfriends (a few from Coqualeetza) had moved to Bella Bella to work in the cannery and they offered to share their living facilities with her. Her main objective of the move was to receive the high wages being paid.

Hopie did not regret her move. It was there that she was introduced to Peter Antoine Minnabarriet, an employee of B.C. Packers and an ex-Coqualeetza student.

She had not known him at school; he arrived the year after she left.

Peter was originally a student at St. George's Residential School in Lytton but finished his last year at Coqualeetza so that he could attend Chilliwack High. He had applied himself fully to all the school courses and sports activities and was a school monitor and sergeant in the Coqualeetza Cadets.

Peter Minnabarriet

His ambition, listed in the school annual, was "to be a minister."

Hopie fell for Peter almost immediately. He was remarkably handsome, with thick, black hair, a beautiful smile, and perfect white teeth. She felt completely at ease with him and was particularly attracted to his good manners and high moral standards. They enjoyed spending leisurely hours together, reminiscing and comparing their experiences at Coqualeetza. It wasn't long before she believed that Peter was definitely "the one." After a short courtship, they decided to leave Bella Bella and move to Vancouver together where there would be better living conditions and more opportunities. Everything was certainly looking up for Agnes Hope

Castle. There was one person not pleased about this union, however — Henry Castle. Henry remembered Peter well as a Coqualeetza monitor. He still held a grudge against monitors, and Peter was no exception.

Hopie and Peter stayed with the Andrews family when they arrived in Vancouver. Peter diligently looked for work in the area but to no avail. He became extremely despondent, causing Hopie much stress and worry. In these financially hard times, jobs were scarce and they were rarely offered to Indians. Peter then made his plans. They would go to the courthouse to be married, and then move to The Ranch.

The Minnabarriet ranch, about nine miles from Spences Bridge, was where Peter was raised. He explained to Hopie that there would be plenty of work on the ranch for him, working with his five brothers, and she could help his mother and sister with the domestic chores. Hopie was completely aghast! Despite her bitter, (but hidden) gross disappointment, off they journeyed to Spences Bridge. She secretly prayed that times would improve and they could soon go back to her beloved Vancouver.

The ranch was *home* to Peter but Hopie felt incredibly shy trying to fit in and thought the family didn't approve of her. Peter's mother, Nancy, was a striking, strong, petite woman and was held in exceptionally high reverence by her husband and six children. Her youthful beauty was portrayed in a large, oval-framed portrait hanging on the sitting room wall of the ranch house. She was raised in her native Indian culture, which was highly matriarchal. She was in complete control and in charge of every aspect of the ranch and could ride a horse with great expertise. Peter's father, Louis Minnabarriet, spoke with a strong French accent. French was his first language but he was half French and half native Indian. Since he was not of Indian status, he was legally able to purchase property. He purchased the ranch property in 1904 for $175.00 which comprised 210 acres of Crown Land.

The Minnabarriet ranch was in a beautiful setting, thriving with an abundance of vegetables, many types of fruit trees, and rows and rows of grape vines. Nancy would take the produce to town with her horse and carriage and barter for the dry goods they needed. The Minnabarriets were totally self-sufficient and everyone was well fed.

There were two ranch houses, one original log house, and one newer house with a kitchen. Hopie and Peter lived with Nancy, Louis, and Mary (Peter's sister) in the newer house, where all the family meals were prepared; the brothers lived in the log house.

It was difficult for Hopie to acclimatize to the extremely hot, dry, summer at the ranch. Fortunately, there was a creek behind the house for easy access to water in the summer. In the winter, they hauled their water from the Thompson River, which was just below the property. Hopie cooperated in these conditions as well as she could. She later revealed to Ruth that she hated ranch life, but never told this to Peter.

In May 1931, Hopie delivered a son, Peter Harold, known as Sonny to the family. The nurturing of the baby, to Hopie's dismay, was also in the hands of Nancy, now referred to as *Granny*. Hopie followed all of granny's ideas of feeding and child rearing, but the canned milk that was fed to the baby caused him to become ill and he had to be taken to Vancouver to receive medical attention. He had developed a hard ball of milk in his stomach, which caused some paralysis.

Hopie was overjoyed to be back in Vancouver to care for little Sonny and to be with her family. It was a great relief to live in a house with modern plumbing and not have to haul water. She wrote a letter to Mary, Peter's sister, dated August 1931, describing her time in Vancouver. She had grown close to Mary and had taught her how to read and write. Following is a portion of her letter.

Dear Mary,

Received your letter this morning and was glad you got that first letter I wrote. I was sorry to

hear that your mother was nearly drowned.
Sonny was real happy this morning. He was
smiling and saying, "Goo" to his mother. I think
he will be better after this. Every time he sees
an electric light he kicks and laughs.

Peter, Lily, Tootsie and I went to Stanley Park
last Sunday. We looked at the monkeys and
everything. Then we sat down and listened to
the band playing.

Peter returned to work at the ranch but Hopie stayed in Vancouver months longer than planned, tending to Sonny's health. She would love sitting by the fire, knitting and enjoying the winter rain instead of the bitter, cold days at granny's ranch. When Sonny's health improved, she had to prepare herself, once again, for more ranch life ahead.

Peter obtained a job with the C.P. Railway in 1933, the year their first daughter, Hope Doreen, was born (later called Doreen). The railroad job would cause Peter to be away much of the time but they knew this was a great opportunity. Hopie was able to cope with the chores and motherhood without Peter but felt a great void when he was away from the ranch.

Two years after Doreen was born, another daughter, Carol Kathleen, arrived in December 1934.

Hopie, 1927

Peter and Hopie strolling down
Granville Street, 1930s

Harold (Sonny) Minnabarriet

Henry was anxious to move to a place of his own after leaving Coqualeetza. No matter what he had to do for work, just being away from Coqualeetza was a good life to him. His first job in Vancouver was driving a coal truck and packing the sacks of coal on his back from the truck to the homes. This was an exceptionally burdensome job but he had it down to an art and the route would be finished in no time.

Henry felt he never belonged to, or was accepted by, the Andrews family. He was emotionally attached only to Hopie and Ruth but had also developed a deep attachment to his brother William (Bill). When Bill became of school age, Sophie had planned to send him to Coqualeetza but Henry so adamantly opposed the idea, Sophie finally had to relent.

By 1931, after several years of driving a truck, Henry had saved enough money to carry out his plan to marry his much loved and adored, Dorothy Heisterman. The Heistermans were a religious, hard-working farm family from Manitoba and lived across the street from the Andrews house. As soon as Henry and Dorothy met, they were inseparable.

Dorothy was blonde, petite and highly energetic. She was an experienced hockey player and had been on a women's hockey team in Manitoba. She had a happy nature, enjoyed Henry's humour and got along splendidly with Sophie. Dorothy was, most definitely, Henry's kind of girl.

Shortly after they were married, Dorothy gave birth to their first child, a daughter, named Shirley. By this time, Henry had begun his own shoe repair business in the basement of their rented home. He would ride his bicycle to various upscale neighbourhoods in Vancouver, soliciting business door-to-door, and became so successful that he later opened a shop on Nanaimo Street. He would often receive discarded shoes that he would repair and give to Sophie for herself and the children.

The Castles' quiet life with one daughter ended four years later. In January 1936, a joyous event happened. Dorothy delivered identical twin boys, Donny and Bobby. Henry took any extra work he could and would make clothing for the boys by cutting down used clothes to make two of each for the twins. Sophie and his sisters had taught him to sew and knit during his school years.

They moved to a rented house on Douglas Street in Burnaby and later managed to borrow enough money to purchase the lot next to it — on the corner of Douglas and William Street. But, for the next six years, they would actually live in a converted chicken coop on the empty lot.

Shirley wrote her recollection of those years:

> They rolled in an old shed from a Russian neighbour, which had been previously used as a

chicken coop. They cleaned it up, made it into a two-room bungalow, gave up their rented house and moved in. Henry built a two-hole outhouse and installed it a few yards away. A small wood stove heated the bungalow. A kettle was always sizzling for a fresh cup of tea and there was always an aroma of stew cooking.

They covered the outside with tarpaper and old boards. Dorothy planted a long row of sweet peas to camouflage the tarpaper. They were given a used car seat, which Henry reconstructed into a chesterfield, using bent water pipes for the arms. Kerosene lamps were used for light and bath night was every Saturday in a large round metal tub, heated by the water on the stove. Dorothy would wash clothes outside on a washboard. Inside, clothes would often hang above the stove to dry.

The Castle family shared many happy times with relatives and friends at this little homestead. It was at this time they owned a Jersey cow called Tiny, a couple of goats and a few chickens which kept them in supply of fresh eggs, milk and Sunday dinners. There were always fresh vegetables from the garden and they often churned the cream for fresh butter and whipped cream. Ice cream was often made on the weekends and kept cold by burying it in the sawdust.

Many chickens lost their heads on Sunday for company suppers. One Sunday, I had to hold the chicken's legs while Henry chopped off the head. I reluctantly did this deed and let the legs go after the head was off and the chicken ran around the yard and under the shed with no head. This was a sight to remember. Then I had the job of plucking the feathers off.

They later acquired a horse for each child, another cow, more chickens, and a duck they named Twaddles. This orphaned duck had joined their chicken family, believing he was one of the chickens. A day came when Henry felt it necessary to serve Twaddles for dinner and no one would eat Twaddles, except Henry.

Henry and Dorothy and Shirley, 1933

Henry with twins on Tiny 1941

Dorothy, Shirley, Bobby and Donny, 1938

Bobby and Donny, 1939

Sophie, 1927

Sophie's safe and secure life came to an end in 1931. Like many families during the Depression, the Andrews family became poverty-stricken. Joseph broke his pelvis and shoulder from a bad fall on the job and he could no longer work as a longshoreman.

Sophie and the children temporarily moved to a small, deserted shack on the farm property in Langley owned by Joseph's mother, Ellen, and her second husband. Sophie was able to grow a small vegetable garden but could provide little else for their needs. Dodie recalled not having any shoes to wear to school and there was never enough to eat. Ellen sometimes provided meals for the family at her farmhouse but the invitations did not include Sophie. Ellen had never approved of Sophie's relationship with both her brother, August, and her son, Joseph. There was great tension between them.

Joseph received a small disability cheque, enough for only one to live on, and eventually moved into a rooming house in downtown Vancouver so that Sophie could receive a Relief Cheque ($6.00) as a single mother. He began playing pool, hoping to win a few extra dollars, and continued to give Sophie what he could. With this arrangement, Sophie was able to return to Vancouver and rent another small house in the east end, on Triumph Street. She took occasional jobs in canneries, sometimes out of the Vancouver area, and later worked as a chambermaid at the *luxurious* Sylvia Hotel.

In 1934, the ultimate tragedy struck the family. Sophie and Joseph's much-loved daughter, Kathleen (Tootsie), died at the age of fifteen. What was first thought to be pneumonia was soon diagnosed as galloping consumption (tuberculosis) and she died soon after. Her younger sister, Isabel, recalled that she had been told that Tootsie was *sleeping* in the casket. It was a horrifying memory for Isabel and there was much grief for everyone in the family. Tootsie had been so well loved that a few family members later admitted that she was their favourite sister.

Everything changed for Sophie and the children in the years after Joseph's accident and Tootsie's death. Another woman entered Joseph's life. By 1936, there would never again be another Andrews House.

Kathleen (Tootsie) in Salvation
Army uniform, age 13

Ruth moved into the Andrews house in the summer of 1934 and started searching for work. It was a sad time to start her life in Vancouver, the time of Tootsie's death. She recalled feeling nervous and unsophisticated going out job-hunting for the first time, but was relieved to be hired as a clerk in a downtown insurance office. Unfortunately, there was a catch — a provisional six-month apprenticeship with no pay except *carfare* (bus or tram fare). So, she took housekeeping jobs in the area and walked to and from work, saving the carfare.

Ruth was extremely outgoing and used every chance to go out exploring the city. She and her girlfriend, Marion, from Chilliwack High, would go out on the town together and quite often go downtown to a public dance. This was their favourite Saturday night event. But Ruth felt slightly naughty going to dances because dancing was not allowed at Coqualeetza. (A teacher was once fired for showing them the steps.)

At one of these dances, she began accepting frequent dance proposals from a man named George Golden Smith. He was five years older and appeared to be quite a charming man-about-town. He had a slight build, handsome features and slicked-back, black hair. Although he displayed a rather cocky attitude, she could see he had a kind and gentle nature under the façade. They had very little in common and she did not consider him to be a serious love interest, but agreed to accept his offer of a dinner date. To her, George's smooth dancing skills were his primary attraction. Sophie kept well aware of what her daughters were up to and would sometimes say, "You better watch out for your sister Dodie, she could come and steal your boyfriend away."

Ruth Castle, 1935

George G. Smith, 1935

When they began dating, they would meet in the usual place, under the legendary Birks' Clock, and would often go to a restaurant on Granville Street for dinner. These extravagant restaurant meals were a complete luxury to Ruth, especially having a choice of dessert. George found it highly amusing that she would choose the dessert before the main course.

After several months of courtship, George made up his mind that Ruth would be his wife. Since she had never actually dated anyone and had no real experience in relationships, she was unable to make the commitment and politely turned him down. That rejection was unacceptable to George; he was persistent and tried everything to convince her otherwise. Eventually, one of his former girlfriends telephoned Ruth and pleaded, "George has locked himself in a hotel room and has been there for two days. You *have* to say you'll marry him or he won't ever come out."

Ruth often wondered how George contrived the hotel room ploy. It didn't occur to her that there may have been some partying going on in the hotel room. She was an inexperienced twenty-four-year-old when they married in 1936 and was still exceptionally naïve. Married life was a whole new learning experience for her. She believed sex was rather silly and could not understand what all the fuss was about.

They rented a house in the Kitsilano area with a large suite for Sophie and the Andrews girls. When Ruth became pregnant, they needed more space for the baby and moved on their own to a small house on Trutch Street. It was the end house of three identical houses, close to the gas station where George worked as a mechanic. On an evening when George had had a few too many in the beer parlour, he walked into the wrong house and fell asleep on their chesterfield. Later that evening, the neighbour came over and asked Ruth, "Can you please come and remove your husband who is sleeping in my front room?"

On October 23, 1937, their first daughter, Ruth Marie, was born. From the day she was born, the family would call her Little Ruthie. When she was older, she begged to be called Marie, but to no avail. She would forever be little Ruthie, and was constantly told, "You look just like your mother."

Just over a year later, another baby was expected and I was that baby. This pregnancy was very difficult and Ruth became dreadfully ill. George was so worried about her that he came up with the idea of sending little Ruthie away to stay with his older sister, Anna and her family in Lethbridge, Alberta for a few months until the baby was born. Anna was like a mother to George, and he adored her. Their parents had died at a young age and Anna had become the family matriarch. Most of George's family were strict Mormons, originally from Raymond, Alberta. George was known as the *rebel* of the family and didn't follow the rules of the Mormon religion, especially when it came to drinking and smoking. He always tried to win Anna's approval, so would hide his bad habits when he was with her family.

On October 30, 1939, I was born. Ruth always felt a great amount of guilt for agreeing to send Ruthie to Lethbridge, and admitted in later years that being a wife and mother did not come easily or naturally to her. Her main female role models had all been reserved, practical, spinster schoolteachers.

George and Ruth
Wedding Photo, 1936

Ruth with little Ruthie, 1938   Sandra and Ruthie, age 1 & 3

~oo0oo~

Chapter Eleven:
The War and After

Peter Minnabarriet in Canadian Army uniform, 1941

World War II broke out and Peter was enticed to join the armed forces. Like other Coqualeetza Cadets, he was trained to always be ready and willing to fight for England. He became so adamant that he registered in the Rocky Mountain Rangers as an unmarried man, since married men were not encouraged to enlist.

Before Peter left for training in Toronto and Victoria, Hopie and the children moved from the ranch into the town of Spences Bridge. They rented a small upstairs suite on the main street, paralleling the C.P.R. tracks. Hopie tried not to agonize over Peter's going to war and decided to concentrate only on making a good life for her children. She was relieved to finally leave the ranch and to register the children in the public school.

The children were well prepared for public school. When Harold became of school age and they were still living at the ranch, Hopie sent for correspondence courses to home-school the children. She dressed them appropriately for school and conducted a strictly disciplined classroom, recess bell and all. Bells were important at Coqualeetza and she trained them as she was trained.

While Peter was in training in Toronto in the summer of 1941, Hopie sent the children to the ranch and travelled to Toronto to visit him. This was the first time she had ever been out of British Columbia. Being alone with Peter in Toronto was an exciting and romantic time, but they did not know then just how long they would soon be apart. A short time later, Peter received the call to be sent overseas for combat.

It was a struggle for Hopie to be on her own in Spences Bridge. To supplement her measly army allowance, she took a job as a dishwasher in a café. She once received a 15-cent tip from a customer there. It was the only tip she ever received in her life. She never forgot it.

With Peter gone, Harold became the man of the house. His main job was to chop the wood and look after the stove; the girls did housework. Harold was also in charge of strictly monitoring the girls' curfew. They didn't know why they had a curfew; there was really no reason to have one in Spences Bridge. During the winter, they would all enjoy ice-skating on a shallow area of the Thompson River. They listened to the radio shows in the evening and kept up-to-date on all the war news. Hopie relied on her religious faith to get them through those many, worrisome days.

Hopie at the ranch with
Doreen and Carol, 1936

Peter and Hopie
in Toronto, 1941

Toronto, 1941

The children earned money by picking wild asparagus and selling it to the local restaurant. With the profits, they would buy wool to knit socks to go along with the dry goods and cigarettes for Peter's care package. Hopie loved to crochet, but could not afford to buy crochet cotton, so she would pull apart a newly crocheted doily and re-do it, over and over again. During the summer months, they would go on hikes in the hills or walk about a mile to the local swimming lake. Every evening at five o'clock the children would go to the railway station and wait for the train so they could wave at the engineer and passengers. Then it was time to go home for supper.

Spences Bridge, railroad bridge in forefront

Children in Spences Bridge would often meet at the school playground to play various games, including their favourite, kick the can. They would arrive on bikes, walk, or ride their horse. Doreen recalled being saved by her cousin Percy (Peter's nephew) when she tried riding a boy's horse and it suddenly went into a gallop and raced down the road. Percy rode up beside her, threw his arm around her waist, and gallantly pulled her onto his horse.

Hopie always felt like she was more English than Indian but didn't feel completely comfortable in either culture. Because of her appearance, people usually assumed she was Indian. She told us of the day two tourists were passing through Spences Bridge and used sign language to her, enquiring about a location for swimming. Because of their sincere efforts, she did not want to embarrass them and felt she had no choice but to answer them in sign language, pointing to the river and slowly saying, "w-a-t-e-r."

It was six long years from the day Peter enlisted in the army until he came home in 1946. Time had changed everyone in many ways. The little children he had left had become grown and it was an enormous adjustment for the whole family. Perhaps more so for Harold; he had been the man of the house for six years.

The war was extremely hard on Peter. The nightmares of the horrors he witnessed constantly haunted him. He would go out for long walks at night, not being able to sleep. Hopie was deeply concerned about the effect the war had on her husband and would often go with him, but he would never divulge to her the memories of what he had seen. The war had changed him considerably. This was a strange and difficult time for the family but they eventually began to share some good times together, getting reacquainted and helping Peter through the healing process.

Peter was re-hired as roadmaster by the C.P.R. and they moved into a house by the river, right next to the bridge, facing the C.N.R. tracks. This was the other end of the bridge from town.

When my sister and I were children, we spent two weeks in the summer with the Minnabarriets in this house, just after Peter came home from the war. They would fill a large tub with water in the front yard for us to sit in for relief from the blazing heat. Our mother gave each of us two dollars for spending money and my sister spent every cent on popsicles. Uncle Pete gave us our first cup of coffee and we felt quite grown up. (Looking back, I believe it was Postum.) We spent a few of the days swimming in the cold Thompson River. Auntie Hopie would put one of us on her back and swim, giving us a thrilling ride. She was the strongest and most expert swimmer we knew. I recall being horrified when I saw a bloodsucker on her leg while she was standing by the water in her bathing suit. She just laughed when she saw it, totally unconcerned.

We played with a little boy named Corky who used to lie under the railway tracks in a hole and watch the trains pass over him. I always believed we tried this too, but my sister didn't recall doing this. It may have been a false memory or a nightmare but I was a bit of a show-off at that age so I'm pretty sure I did. The small, railroad town of Spences Bridge was like an entirely different world than ours in Vancouver. Now, when I get a whiff of sagebrush or hear the sound of crickets, I always think of Spences Bridge in 1946.

It was great fun when we were taken on a trip to granny's ranch and rode in her horse-drawn carriage. Granny lifted us onto a tame old horse and took us for our first horseback ride. We thought she was wonderful, and she could jump on a horse like a real cowboy.

Two years after Peter returned from the war, the C.P.R. transferred him to Ashcroft, B C. The Aylmer's Tomato Company cannery was thriving at this time in Ashcroft and Hopie and the children all obtained a part-time job there at one time or another. They purchased a house in town, away from the railway tracks.

Hopie and Peter were proud of their children. Unlike many parents, their children did not cause them any concern during their teenage years. Doreen and Carol were beautiful girls and Carol was often told she resembled the movie star, Cyd Charisse. She was once asked to be Miss May Day without even seeking the job, much to Doreen's chagrin. To top it all off, Doreen recalled, Carol had a gorgeous circular skirt and was always twirling in it.

Harold was also good-looking and had a beautiful singing voice. He and Peter loved music and spent hours together listening to records, singing, and playing their banjos and guitars. Peter learned to play a banjo and guitar at Coqualeetza and taught his skills to Harold. One of my girlfriends had a crush on Harold after watching him sing a solo at a family wedding.

The Minnabarriet children had happy childhoods in Spences Bridge and Ashcroft. It didn't occur to them to feel deprived of anything. Small town life was all they knew. Doreen doesn't recall any racism, but she remembered a woman once calling her family *Bohunks*.

Doreen   Harold   Carol

Carol and Doreen Minnabarriet, c. 1947

Minnibarriet house in Spences Bridge -
West end (CNR side) of the bridge, 2001

↑

Bridge

Carol, Doreen, Harold,
Hopie and Peter, 1946

"Went camping by
horseback. Slept under
the stars at Venables
Valley. Hopie made
bannock over a
campfire."

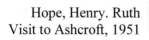

Hope, Henry. Ruth
Visit to Ashcroft, 1951

Doreen, 1953

Carol, 1953

Doreen, c. 1950

Harold (date unknown)

During the beginning of the war, both Henry and Bill registered in the armed forces. Bill was accepted, but Henry was not (possibly because of his small stature and flat feet). Henry was able to obtain a job at the shipyards as a riveter on large battleships which awarded him a much higher income than his shoe repair business. He was soon able to purchase the building material he needed to build their dream house. After just over a year on the job, he had a debilitating accident. He fell from the scaffolding and badly injured his neck and spine. He spent months in hospital and it was thought that he would never walk again. He was placed in a body cast from his neck to his thighs and remained in the cast long after his release from the hospital. After extended therapy, he was able to begin walking.

This accident, and being in a body cast, did not deter Henry from carrying out his vision — he took it as the perfect opportunity to begin building his house. Dorothy and the children helped with the heavy lifting, other members of their families participated in the construction, and Henry became known as Major Hoople. By 1945, the house was complete enough to move in. "But there were parts that were never finished," Shirley recalled. "It was an on-going project."

Castle house: 3920 William St, Burnaby, B.C.

The house had a modern, open floor plan with three bedrooms and a large kitchen and pantry. Everyone was elated, especially Dorothy — they *finally* had indoor plumbing. They had lived in The Coop for a total of six years.

A job advertisement by Crystal Dairies came to Henry's attention during the latter stages of the house construction. They were seeking a milkman for a horse-and-wagon milk route in the area. It was the perfect job for him and he grasped the opportunity. Shirley wrote:

> Everyone knew Henry the Milkman. He rode
> his bike from his home in Burnaby to the
> Crystal Dairy barns at 4:00 in the morning each
> day and arrived home at 2:00 in the afternoon.

Dorothy would diligently help him with his bookwork.

He had a way with horses, and they responded well to him. The horse knew the route well and would stop automatically at each house call.

Shirley and the twins helped on the milk route during weekends, sometimes taking along a friend, and their reward would be a pint of chocolate milk.

When Shirley attended a high school reunion years later, her friend commented that the trips in the milk wagon were one of the highlights of her childhood in Burnaby.

Eventually the old horse-and-wagon had to be updated to a truck. Bobby and Donny continued helping Henry and began learning to drive. On a day when Henry was too ill to do the route, he sat in the back and supervised while one little twin pushed the floor pedals, the other steered.

A great surprise happened to the Castles in 1953. Dorothy, then in her forties, became pregnant. She was highly perturbed at Henry for her condition and would no longer allow him in her bed. "It wasn't my fault." he explained, "She just helped herself!" This baby was their much-loved son, Herbert, known to the family as Herbie. Shirley had already left home and the twins, Bob and Don, were 17 years old.

Herb admits that he was spoiled and was tied to his mother's apron strings. He usually felt like an only child. Henry and Dorothy also spoiled the twins, and Henry would say in later years: "They were spoiled rotten — and then they were just rotten."

It was great fun for us to visit Uncle Henry's house when we were children. We were not allowed to read comic books at home and the twins had boxes and boxes of comic books, including all the latest editions. Their mischievous ways kept us so highly entertained, it was always well worth the long, smelly tram rides to Burnaby.

Shirley, Dorothy, Donny and Bobby, 1941

Dorothy and Henry, 1943

Bobby, Donny and Shirley, 1943

Bobby, Ruthie, Donny and Sandra, 1943
Ruthie and the twins were
sometimes mistaken for triplets.

Henry and twins in homemade horse cart, riding in Burnaby, 1943

Shirley's graduation photo, 1950

Bob and Don, 1956

Dorothy and Herbie, 1953

Herb, 1971

Ruth was rather child-like as a young mother. She had an extremely happy, fun-loving nature and enjoyed playing outside with us. She was an expert at skipping rope and the neighbourhood children would often come over and ask, "Can your mom come out and play?"

She constantly practiced the piano and played for our tap dance class in exchange for our tap lessons. My sister and I had vivid memories of our elderly tap dance teacher in her heavy navy tunic, black stockings and tap shoes, shouting, **"Shuffle down, shuffle down, shuffle down, one two!"** while our mother pounded away at the piano. Ruth loved movies, particularly English movies, and took us to many of the classics shown at the Studio Theatre on Granville Street. George could never understand how she could stand in line for hours, just to see a movie.

By the mid-forties, George had joined the union and worked out-of-town on construction as a pipe-fitter. When he came home from a long-term job, he usually had grown a beard and we hardly recognized him. He would flex his muscles, telling us he was "the strongest man in the world" and we believed him. I always wanted to be like him — the boy he never had. I would love to dig up jars of worms for our fishing trips and chase my sister with snakes, just as a boy would do. I ate lots of spinach because he told me it would help grow hair on my chest.

George posing at Trutch Street house, 1943

3543 West 5th Ave

It was a thrilling day in 1945 when we moved to the big house on West 5th Avenue in Vancouver. It had an upstairs with two bedrooms and a basement with scary, hidden passages. The back yard was unfenced and extended out to an empty lot, perfect for building forts. The house was about forty years old and could have been purchased at the time for less than $5,000.

Growing up in the Kitsilano area was ideal for us. We would ride our bikes to Jericho Beach in the summer and stay all day and nobody ever seemed to worry about us being on our own. Our primary school, Bayview, was just two blocks away. To me, it was the perfect childhood.

During the war, our house was often a gathering place for parties and piano sing-a-longs. They would sing all the old favourites, like "Irene Good Night," over and over again, while we were trying to sleep. I also recall being taken to other homes and sleeping wherever they could find a space; then sometimes being dragged or carried home half asleep. Our mom's mile-high apple pies and homemade bread were usually baking in the oven but the main meals were usually cooked by Grandma or our dad. When sliced bread became popular, we would ask for store-bought bread because we were embarrassed of our homemade bread sandwiches at school. We would often trade our mom's beautifully hand-sewn or crocheted doll clothes for cheap, manufactured clothes.

When Sophie and her youngest daughter, Frankie, were on their own in Vancouver in the early 1940s, they moved to Spences Bridge to live with Hopie. One day, on her way to school, Frankie fell on a railway track and struck her head. This seemingly minor fall later turned out to be devastating. When they returned to Vancouver to live with us soon after her fall, Frankie suddenly collapsed and was admitted to hospital in a coma. This resulted in some slight brain damage and she remained in hospital for over six months. She was later required to wear a leg brace and Sophie could no longer send her to school.

Sophie and Frankie lived with us on 5th Avenue for a number of years and Frankie became like an older sister to us. Sophie looked after us while Ruth was working and George was away on construction. If there was ever a problem between Ruth and George, Sophie would often side with George. She seemed to favour the male in the house and would cater and cook especially for him. By the early 1950s, Frankie got married and Sophie was alone.

Ruth began questioning her religious upbringing and studied different religions to find one she felt she could faithfully follow. She became a Jehovah's Witness for a short time and also studied the Mormon and Baptist religions. She played the organ at the Baptist Church where we were sent to Sunday school and C.G.I.T. (Canadian Girls in Training). She wavered on the religion issue for some time but finally withdrew from all. She eventually came to realize that her heart was with the philosophy of her native Indian heritage.

Dr. Raley kept in touch with many of his ex-students and visited Ruth fairly often. My sister and I were fascinated with his proper manners and English accent and we thought he was a medical doctor. We loved it when he came to visit — he would shake our hand and secretly slip us a chocolate bar.

Those good old days of mom in the kitchen came to an end in 1946. She had dutifully fulfilled her job as a housewife and stay-at-home mother until we were both registered in school and then began her dream of working with Indian people. Through Guy Williams, then a member of the Native Brotherhood and an ex-Coqualeetza student, Ruth obtained a job as their secretary. The Native Brotherhood had recently begun publishing an Indian newspaper called, *The Native Voice*. That was to be the beginning of some long, hard days of work to come for Ruth.

The Native Voice paper took all of her time and energy. She was working day and night and would often go on speaking tours. Some family members later admitted to not claiming her as a relative because they did not want to reveal their Indian blood. The day after one of her radio interviews, a boy at school called my sister a *squaw.* It was upsetting for her, but there were many more demeaning names used freely in those years.

Sandra and Ruthie
Age 10 and 12

Ruth became editor of the paper in 1947 and was becoming quite well-known in Vancouver. There were times we would be taken to a meeting or celebration where there would be Indians in ceremonial dress, singing and dancing. We would be fascinated, but also a bit frightened. This was the age of Hollywood cowboy and Indian movies at Saturday matinees and these movies had a great effect on children. The Indians were mostly depicted as savages or the enemy. When we played Cowboys and Indians in the neighbourhood, I always enjoyed playing the Indian.

It was rather unusual for mothers to be business-women in the forties. My friend commented, years later, that she greatly admired our mother — barely five feet tall, small waist and feet, dressed in her smart business suit going downtown to work every day.

In Ruth's box of treasures is an autographed photo of the young, beautiful Lena Horne. Ruth had interviewed her for an article in the Native Voice and they discussed matters of segregation, such as the fact that Ms. Horne, like native Indians in Canada, could not register in a hotel. She told Ruth she had an Indian grandmother. During the 1940s and 50s many African American entertainers came to Vancouver because of the thriving night clubs and when Hogan's Alley in the Strathcona area still existed.

The magazine section of The Vancouver Sun of September 11, 1948, featured Ruth and her work with The Native Voice; her photo filled the entire section cover. I was so excited about this that I gathered my friends in the neighbourhood to perform a street parade. We had tambourines and drums and marched down the middle of 5th Avenue. I led the marching parade with the magazine cover stuck through a long stick, holding it high in the air. Then I heard, "Sandra, come in the house right now!" I was in trouble and I didn't know why.

Following are two extracts from newspaper clippings:

Voice for Others, by Margaret Francis

The editor of America's largest Indian newspaper, *The Native Voice*, is Dresden-like brunette Ruth Smith, an attractive 34-year-old Vancouver housewife. When the majority of Indian women, wounded by snubs and discrimination in a white man's world, crept back to their Indian homes, Ruth set out to conquer that world. At Coqualeetza school, near Sardis, B.C., Ruth excelled at sports. She led her classes. She won high honours when she took the Toronto Conservatory examinations in Pianoforte.

She took a business course, and in Vancouver held a good position as a secretary until she married George Smith. But as soon as her two little girls, Ruth and Sandra, now 10 and eight, passed their baby days, she became restless for self-expression.

When *The Native Voice* was founded in December 1946, she joined the staff, first as secretary and then as editor. The staff is Indian, and Big White Owl of Toronto is associate editor. Her correspondents are on reservations and in Indian settlements across

Canada. "Few white people realize the problems that face the Indians and their cruel poverty," she says. "We've been able to draw attention to these and see signs of a changing attitude. On the other hand, we want to give our people a pride in their own culture and traditions."

Mrs. Smith has a dash of English and Irish herself, which has given her her clear Irish skin, but she's more proud of her Indian blood.

TRIBUTE, Vancouver 'Woman of The Day'

Mrs. Eleanor Roosevelt has sent a present of a silver tray to a Vancouver woman for being one of this continent's distinguished women. The recipient, Mrs. Ruth Smith, is the woman who was editor of The Native Voice, monthly Indian paper, in '47 and '48.

She was the subject of the 'Woman of the Day' radio program prepared by Mrs. Roosevelt and Anna Roosevelt.

A member of the Salish tribe, Mrs. Smith resigned from her newspaper job, and is now working on plans for an Indian centre in Vancouver to try to find jobs and housing for Indians.

Ruth's article, entitled, "Just Another Damned Indian" created a positive response from many readers. Following is an extract from her article:

> Many books have been written on the habits, general characteristics and art of our people, but does Canada know about the philosophy, the gentle humour, the spiritual quality and the heart of the Indian people? Has Canada ever cared?
>
> A wonderful way of life is fading and the final stage is epitomized in our aged people today. Their eyes have seen the end of so-called *primitive* life and they see *civilized* life; their faces relax into resigned, kindly lines and their eyes speak of suffering.
>
> I remember as a child visiting in a home that must have been very poor but I did not see that then, I only saw two very old women sitting on the floor. I remember their hands, kind, gentle and it seemed to me big with love, and their voices crooning softly as they spoke.
>
> Do you think these people watch what is happening to the young without bitter suffering?
>
> Just as you, they saw their young men march to war and be killed. Their agony is not one whit

less than the agony in your heart, yet they suffer indignities and pangs of hunger in their bellies.

What of the mothers and fathers today? They have not the comfort of surety. They have been told in every look, gesture and the law that they are inferior, in so many words, "you damned Indian." That is no uncommon term; it has been said over and over. You cannot know, you can't begin to know what it does to you, this feeling of dreadful uncertainty, this uprooting of a people and their beliefs; the ridicule, the slurs until one pain is locked away, and then another. You say, "Forget it, put it on the shelf and take if off only when it can act as a spur." You can't do that when it becomes a part of you. You can only put on a mask, thank God for a good sense of humour and be yourself when you are with your own people.

The Native Voice is asking for equal status and opportunities for native Indians in representation, education, better housing and facilities.

Schools for Indians are entirely insufficient. Consideration of money has been such a devilish factor that, except for a very limited number, our children graduate with not enough education to hurdle the reservation fences.

In the past six years, hospitals for TB patients have been erected in different parts of Canada. They are filled to capacity. The work done by those in charge cannot be too highly praised, but nothing is being done on the reserves in health education, and so tuberculosis spreads.

Superior warfare subdued the Indian and he was given a little piece of land, and certain laws were passed to *protect* him. Then he was conveniently forgotten.

The most devastating law, that of making him a minor, still exists. This law prevents him from pre-empting land, from borrowing money to build a home, from borrowing to buy a tractor to till his land or improve the roads, from entering into a business contract, from voting, etc.

The Indian is subjected to taxation without benefit; there is no old-age pension, mother's pension, or social security.

Many more discouragements arise from these major injustices, but the Indian cannot say one word, as he is not represented in Ottawa.

The Native Voice produced interesting and informative papers concerning native Indian people in Canada and the U.S. and Ruth was proud of the job she had accomplished. Although she was entirely devoted to her work, she was exhausted and felt she needed to stop working and concentrate on her family. This was an agonizing decision for her — one that she may have later regretted — but during these times, it was the right thing to do. Her marriage had become strained.

When my sister and I were in our early teens and beginning junior high, our mother was often worried by some of our activities. There was little similarity between being a teenager at Coqualeetza and being a teenager at Kitsilano High. Our interests were entirely foreign to her and our behaviour completely mystified her. Not knowing how to handle us, she began studying child psychology and having many consultations with her girlfriend, Bea, a professional psychologist.

In 1953, our lives took a sudden change. George was sent to work in Kimberley, B.C. and we were forced to move with him. One of the reasons for this decision was to remove us from influences they deemed inappropriate for us. We suspected that Bea had to be involved in this decision. Changing schools from *cool* Kitsilano High to small-town Kimberley High was a total culture shock; we thought our lives were over. After a year in Kimberley, then it was off to Kamloops for another construction job at the Royalite Refinery. Kamloops, in our minds, was only a slight step towards reality.

Our first home in Kamloops was a rental cabin at Riverside Park. It was great fun living there but, unfortunately, it was not to last. We then moved on to an apartment downtown above the Silver Grill Restaurant with a view of the Greyhound Bus Depot. Eventually, we rented a house on Dominion Street quite near the high school. My four years at Kam High were some of my fondest memories. I have kept many lifelong friends from those high school years.

Ruth and George's main choice of recreation in Kamloops was fishing and Kamloops was the ideal place for this. They acquired new friends and Ruth went back to work in an insurance office. Within a few years they had an empty nest and decided to take a chance and become adventurous — they applied for their green cards and moved to California. Two of George's brothers lived there and offered them a business opportunity.

The Vancouver Sunday Sun
Magazine, slightly torn cover,
Sep.1948

Silver Tray presented to Ruth
as 'Woman of the Day' by
Mrs. Eleanor Roosevelt

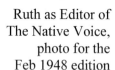

Ruth as Editor of
The Native Voice,
photo for the
Feb 1948 edition

Ruthie 1955

Sandra 1956

George at Royalite
Refinery in Kamloops

Ruth and George
partying in Kamloops

~~ooOoo~

Part Three

Chapter Twelve:
The Coqualeetza Reunion

Top: Ed Kelly, Peter Minnabarriet, Dolly Kelly
Bottom: Hope Minnabarriet, Ruth Smith, 1972

The Coqualeetza school reunion of 1972 was a memorial, historical event, filled with sentiment. For a few, it had been about sixty years since being at the school. Miss Bailey (Culinary Arts/Matron) and Miss Adams (Sewing) were still living and attended the reunion with great enthusiasm. Mrs. E. Charlton, Dr. Raley's daughter, was also in attendance.

Ruth's inspiration to plan the reunion began soon after she and George returned to B.C. after nine years in California. Ruth was yearning to be back in touch with old friends and called her dear friend, Dolly, with the idea. It had been almost forty years since their graduation from Coqualeetza and they were both extremely anxious to take on this enormous task. It would take at least two years to accomplish. Many ex-students were living on the Queen Charlotte Islands and were difficult to contact. After much hard work and organization, it finally came about and was held at the old Coqualeetza school building in Sardis.

Since Ruth didn't drive, I was available to be her chauffeur and had the honour of attending this reunion. I was anxious to go and, of course, was interested in meeting her first love, Oliver (Skinny) Adams. I definitely detected a sparkle in their eyes when they saw each other. During the evening, I overheard Oliver enjoying telling stories of how daring it was for the boys to sneak over to the girls' side. This was not the first time

Ruth and Oliver had seen each other over the years. When Ruth worked for the Native Brotherhood and The Native Voice, they had often been in touch and always remained good friends. In later years, Oliver Adams became Chief at Skidegate.

As a note of interest, Dolly Kelly (Delavina Allard) married Ed Kelly, another former Coqualeetza student. Ed became a famous old-timer in Sardis, retiring from barbering in 1993 at the age of 92. His haircut prices never increased from $6.00. His shop was attached to their home on Vedder Road in Sardis. Ed Kelly was Canada's oldest working barber as well as Canada's first official native Indian barber. Ed's sister was Martha, as in, "Think you're bigger than..."

During the reunion, Ed Kelly recalled:

> When I was a baker boy, they had a Dutch oven
> in the old school and heated it with cordwood.
> To test the baking temperature, we would stick
> an arm in the oven and count to five. If we had
> to pull out our arm before the count was
> finished, it was too hot. This was our
> homemade gauge.

The *COMBO* newspaper, printed by the Mission in Canada, asked Ruth to write an article on the reunion for their summer 1973 edition.

On the Reunion day, the sun shone — and the time is now. But time got mixed up when we arrived in Sardis and drove to Coqualeetza, our old school. There is something about sounds and places that can transport you immediately. It was as if a time machine got all mixed up because it didn't take you all the way back to your childhood; the place was the same, but somehow different with the addition to the buildings when it was a hospital. The atmosphere was friendly but without the noisy sounds of children: the people were the same, but changed also. After all, the time span since school days was thirty-five, forty-five, and a few as much as sixty years.

It was an exciting day. At first there was an air of tentative shyness which wore off as we recognized the faces of those we grew up with; many seemed to be looking for their special chums, meeting and exchanging memories, looking at old photographs and Annuals. It was just not long enough! ... The Banquet was filled with camaraderie and the speeches evoked nostalgia. I believe momentarily we touched souls.

It left me with a strange unrest. Sadness and time seemed all mixed up. The deepest impression was something about our old people, what was it? I think it was a thought, a reasoning that had filtered through the confusing years that followed school days.

As I observed our people in their eighties, it was apparent that the influence of the old culture is there; they are peculiarly Indian, and I was very proud. Why? They have a lovely quietness about them, they have dignity and they have integrity. I wish we had cherished them more, listened to them more.

Dolly & Ruth at Reunion

Ruth and Dolly dressed in school day era clothes, with former teacher looking on.

Coqualeetza Today

The **Coqualeetza Hospital** continued operating until its closing in 1969. The building was also used as an important facility for non-Indian people. Virtually every kind of organization made use of Coqualeetza — the Foresters, IODE, the suffragettes and even members of the prohibition movement.

The Department of Public Works took it over in 1974 and, in the same year, leased the main brick complex (formerly the hospital) to the Department of National Defence. The Stó:lō Nation received control of all the outside smaller buildings — The Big House, Salish Weaving, Snookwa Hall and the two houses located at the rear, namely the library and the area Indian council centre.

The Coqualeetza buildings are now the Stó:lō Service Agency, the political amalgamation of eleven Stó:lō communities providing services to the Stó:lō and Aboriginal communities throughout S'olh Temexw.

Coqualeetza building, 2002

Coqualeetza building

Principal's house, 2002 (gift shop before being demolished)

New Coqualeetza building addition

~oo0oo~

Chapter Thirteen:
'til we Meet at Dawn

Hopie and Ruth on a street in Ashcroft, late 1980s

Sophie Andrews

Sophie was usually able to live with one of her children and rarely lived alone. She could fit herself into any home with ease. She was so accustomed to living with others, she would sometimes just show up if she felt she was needed to help with a family crisis or a new baby. Her elder

Sophie, 1961

years were spent with her daughter, Dodie, in Courtenay, B.C. Sophie died in 1965 at the age of seventy-five.

Henry George, Sophie's brother, died in 1964. According to Sophie, Henry's wife never approved of her or her family and their families did not know each other. She was proud, and often bragged, that Henry was chosen to engineer the train for Queen Elizabeth and King George VI on their tour of British Columbia in 1939. Sophie was a true monarchist and always kept up-to-date on the lives of the Royal Family. Her only indulgence was her love of shoes, of which she had many.

Sophie rarely spoke of her childhood or her marriage to August. It was only quite recently that our family knew All Hallows had separate schools for Indian and white girls. She also never discussed her relationship with her mother, Lucy George.

Joseph Andrews

Joseph managed to purchase a small fishing boat, something he had always dreamed of, and fishing became his life. He continued to stay in touch with Sophie through the years and they remained close friends.

Joseph at Tranquille Hospital

He contracted T.B. in 1955 and stayed in the Tranquille T.B. Hospital in Kamloops for two years. He later lived with his daughter, Frankie, in North Vancouver.

Joseph fished as long as he was able. He died in 1968 at the age of eighty-four.

The Andrews Siblings

William (Bill)

Doris (Dodie)

Isabel

Frances (Frankie)

August Castle

Before August died in 1969, my mother and I visited him at the old Castle house in Yale. He was about a hundred years old at the time. His only apparent disability was that he had weak legs and could barely walk, but seemed healthy and able in every other way. It was amusing to see him still being flirtatious with the ladies in his presence. He even flirted with me. My mother was never impressed with August but, by this time, it didn't really matter.

It took many years for Hope, Henry and Ruth to outwardly discuss August's other families. Many of us were not aware of all the half-siblings they had. The whole August Castle situation was too painful for Ruth and Hopie to discuss openly and was usually just whispered about.

After Sophie left Yale, August married Emma, his travelling companion, and they had three daughters. He purchased a house from his son-in-law, Francis Creighton, which is now the Yale Historic Museum. When I recently visited this museum, and mentioned that August Castle was my grandfather, a museum employee asked me if I knew an Emma. She said the museum employees often feel Emma's presence in the house.

Castle House (pictured with Louise Ward, Mary Alice Ward,
David J. Creighton, Alice Malathia Jane, Moses Dundas, and
Francis Henry, early 1900s

Castle House – now the Yale Historic Museum, July 2002

Besides the death of his parents, August mourned many family members during his life. In 1915 his son, Frank, drowned in the Fraser River at the age of fifteen; both of his brothers died in 1938 — Alfred was struck and killed by a Vancouver streetcar on a Kitsilano trestle and

Castle siblings (date unknown)
Alfred
August   Ellen   Martin

Martin died on a C.P.R. train on route to a Vancouver hospital. His sister, Ellen, also died in 1938 and his daughter, Margaret, tragically died at a young age in 1944. August also outlived his four, much younger, wives.

Following is a copy of an article from The Vancouver Sun, dated May 8, 1969:

LAST SPIKE DRIVEN

CPR Pioneer Dies At 105 Years

A man who was present when the last spike of the Canadian Pacific Railway was driven is dead at the age of 105.

August Castle worked on the last stretch of construction of the CPR between Yale and Lytton and was present when The Last Spike was driven at Craigellachie, meeting point of the trans-continental CPR on Nov. 7, 1885.

Mr. Castle attained fame as a posse leader and bandit hunter and besides working for the railway, also prospected in the upper Fraser Valley and Fraser Canyon.

During his lifetime, he worked part-time as a government–appointed special policeman protecting the CPR from outlaws.

LED POSSES

He also led posses which took part in manhunts for such legendary B.C. criminals as train robber Bill Miner, and murderers Paul Spintlum and Moses Paul at the turn of the century.

His love of prospecting paid off when he was one of the ones to stake a claim in the Giant Mascot (then Pacific Nickel) mine near Hope. He received $10,000 when he sold his claim in the mid-1920s.

One of his most treasured possessions was a gold watch chain studded with more than a dozen large gold nuggets he found in the Fraser River.

Mr. Castle was born in Victoria, where his father owned three bakeries and moved to New Westminster at the age of 13 when his parents died.

BEGINNING OF CAREER

In 1880, he and his brother Martin travelled by the paddle-wheeler Beaver up the Fraser River to Yale to begin his railway and prospecting adventures.

His house in Yale was built on foundations of the former residence of Judge Matthew Begbie, known as The Hanging Judge.

Hope Minnabarriet

Hopie and Peter were transferred from Ashcroft to the Kettle Valley Railway in Penticton in 1953. They purchased a house on the same street as their son, Harold, and enjoyed many retirement years in the Okanagan.

In 1975, they suffered the most devastating loss; their youngest daughter, Carol, died of cancer. During her years of illness, they spent much of their time travelling to Kamloops, where Carol lived.

Peter died in 1981 and was buried in the Minnabarriet family cemetery on the hill next to granny's ranch. Throughout his life, he always conducted himself on the straight and narrow in every way, never diverting an inch. His method of paying bills was done the old-fashioned way — personally, in cash. Hopie would complain that any trips they planned would always have to coincide with bill-paying due dates.

Hopie was never able to get over how handsome she thought Peter was and she mentioned it often. He treated her so well after returning from the war that she considered herself to be spoiled. Her gentle and gracious manner made it easy to spoil her; it would have been difficult to treat her in any other way. She suffered some racial discrimination in her life but always seemed to quietly accept anything that came her way. Ruth often worried about this, knowing it was indeed painful for her.

Hopie and Ruth were well known for their giggling together, usually in the bathroom. This was such usual behaviour that their husbands learned to ignore it. Ruth often complained about the fact that Hopie had no wrinkles and her hands looked as though she had never done a day's work. When Ruth began losing her hearing in her elder years, she could not hear Hopie's extraordinarily softly-spoken voice on the telephone, which was very frustrating for them both. Even when it was necessary, Hopie could not raise her voice.

Peter and Hopie had greatly looked forward to attending Peter's reunion of the B.C. Dragoons, which was to take place in Holland in 1982, a year after Peter died. Hopie undertook to fulfil this commitment and travelled to Holland with her daughter, Doreen. The people in Holland felt great gratitude for the rescue of their country by the Canadians during the war and Peter was well remembered by a few of the old-timers. Hopie found the trip most memorable and said she was treated like a queen.

Hopie lived independently in an apartment in Ashcroft near Doreen after Peter died. She was often seen entering or leaving the Ashcroft Legion, enjoying their social activities. Doreen was concerned how this may appear to others — a drinking establishment was the last place one would expect to see Hopie. Of course, she never took a drink; she was much too proper.

The Coqualeetza motto, "No Backward Step" remained instilled in Hopie's mind and, unlike Ruth, she did not have a great interest in her Indian heritage. She never lost her Christian faith and regularly attended church. In a tribute to Hopie on her eightieth birthday, Ruth wrote:

> Hope has lived her many years with quiet
> courage. I can say I have never known her to
> respond to any situation with anything but
> kindness and gentleness; she deemed not to
> deviate from the standards she set for herself.
> She is a True Lady.

Hopie died on February 17, 1991 at the age of eighty-three.

Hopie, with Ruth's granddaughter, 1983

Hope Minnabarriet, 1985

Hopie in Veendam, Holland,
standing with Mayor

Copy of The Journal newspaper photo,
entitled 'A shy, gentle woman'
under Personality of the Week,
January 1989

Root Cellar   Fruit Stands

The Minnabarriet ranch was once known as 89 Mile House on the Cariboo Wagon Road. In 1924, the road was widened and renamed the Fraser Canyon Highway, now called the Trans Canada Highway. Nancy continued to live and farm on the property until 1970. Several of the buildings were destroyed by fire. There are no buildings left standing today.

Nancy Minnabarriet (Granny) as an elder, c. 1955

Abandoned Minnabarriet log house

Ruth Smith

Ruth and George were anxious to return to B.C. in 1969. The business venture they had been asked to join with his brothers in California had failed. It was difficult starting over; they were then in their fifties.

George re-joined the union and went to work at Mica Dam, near Revelstoke. They paid a down payment on a small lot in Chase, B.C. with a view of the Little Shuswap Lake and then starting saving for a house. Within a few years, George was not well enough to continue working.

Ruth was eager to get involved with the local Indian affairs and became secretary to Robert Manual of the Neskonlith Indian Band in Chase. She worked hard for the band and took great enjoyment in the work and being involved with the people and their activities. For several years, George and his dog, Fifi, (known as his mistress,) would drive Ruth to and from her job on the reserve. Ruth was never able to obtain a driver's licence. "She would speed up around corners," George explained. When Ruth's secretarial days were over, he would enjoy sitting on the deck of their house and watch her labouring in the garden. "Your mother is pushing rocks around again," he would say, shaking his head. He tried hard many times to kick his life-long habit of smoking. The day he announced he had finally quit, we all gathered for a family celebration dinner while he sat quietly in the basement having a cigarette.

George died in 1982 after a long illness. Ruth had been his only caregiver and found it to be completely exhausting. His illness took most of her energy and the book she had started with a group of friends from Coqualeetza got put aside.

Ruth's deep passion concerning the unjust treatment of the Indian people grew even more through the years. She would have been willing to get back into any kind of work for the people but George's illness and her age prevented her from doing so. She agonized at the stories she heard over the years of the abuse to children in some residential schools.

The following extracts are taken from her notes regarding her thoughts on residential schools, in general, written in 1977:

> When attempting the research, I found there is
> very little from which to draw. The main
> question to me is: why was the education of
> Indian children turned over to the churches for
> so long? It appears it is because the various
> churches had already undertaken on their own
> the education of the children in their area.
> Many non-Indian people are surprised that
> most Indian children did not have the

opportunity to attend public schools, generally speaking, until the late 1950s and early 60s.

I feel the most glaring error practised by the residential schools in Canada was the denial of the children's own language. It was probably done with good intentions, but in a very harsh manner by the use of the strap and sometimes by beatings. It also created an unnatural gap and effectively prevented the closeness and understanding between the generations. It prevented the teaching of the culture by the elders, the telling of our history and legends. This caused a deep sadness among the elderly people and what must have been frustration beyond words.

An aggressive and arrogant society superimposed their culture on ours without trying to understand this land or the people and by allowing no input in the direction of our lives, effectively minimizing the culture and creating a feeling of hopelessness and frustration. This, in turn, nurtured a sense of loss of our identity. It was done at a time when the Indian people had already reached a very high spiritual and creative level.

The present society still has much of this development to reach, such as: the worth of sharing, respect for the land and all living creatures, and the ability to live in harmony with nature.

The young Indians today seem to have sensed that their ancestors had something of value and they are now reaching back to their roots for strength; they feel that they no longer want to follow without question. In their search, they may even find themselves in a position of leadership.

Ruth attended anything of interest she could — every lecture, art show, craft fair and pow wow. In her seventies, she joined Amnesty International, went on a meditation retreat, took up cross-country skiing and slid down the waterslide in Salmon Arm, called The Twister. She continued to be an avid reader and kept up-to-date on worldly and Indian affairs. She kept an open mind to all political views, but continued to be an NDP supporter.

In her elder years, after attending a weekend fair, she brought a young couple home to stay overnight, who were virtual strangers. She wondered why we would question her judgement. It was easily explained. "They were a lovely couple that needed somewhere to sleep."

Ruth's favourite pastime was to have deep discussions on any subject, while serving her homemade scones with butter, homemade jam and cups of tea. The English schoolteachers' influences were obvious in both Hopie and Ruth. She enjoyed the *useful womanly crafts* learned at Coqualeetza — crocheting and knitting — and was an expert in the dying art of tatting lace.

Ruth died on June 28th, 1994 at the age of eighty-two.

Ruth, 1971   Ruth, 1988

George, Fifi and
Ruth in Chase, 1973

Ruth on Twister

Ruthie, Ruth
and Sandra, 1993

Henry Castle

Henry was not ready to conjure up his Coqualeetza memories and did not attend the Coqualeetza reunion in 1972. Getting over a long-held grudge was difficult for him. The cruelty he endured at Coqualeetza was mainly from a few of the boys and one particular teacher. It is not known if these grudges eventually dissipated, but he was soon able to forgive Peter Minnabarriet for being a monitor. He learned later in life that his difficulty in reading and writing was caused by dyslexia.

Henry's children did not know, until they were adults, that he was half native Indian and had lived in a residential school for fourteen years. He seldom discussed his past and believed his children would have better lives if they did not know of their Indian blood. When I asked his daughter, Shirley, why they wouldn't have noticed the obvious Indian appearance of some relatives, she said they didn't think of those things as children and would not have questioned it. As a note of interest, Shirley recently told me that August had visited their home at one time but Henry met him outside. He did not come in the house. Shirley asked her mother who that man was and her mother said, "He's your grandfather."

Henry began working for Dawson Construction in the 1950s as a roller operator building roads. Although the job description required experience, he applied for the job believing it couldn't be much different than driving a truck. He worked for Dawson for thirty-three years, working on many of B.C.'s roads and highways. He was a highly skilled operator and was often called back to work after his retirement. He did not fully retire from this job until he was seventy-three years old. He also trained his son, Don, as an operator.

Dorothy and Herb often accompanied Henry working on the road in the summers, usually camping in their camper at a nearby lake. They all joined the rock club. "Everything was rocks, rocks, rocks," according to Shirley. Henry had a gigantic rock collection and any guests visiting the Castle house were automatically taken to the basement to view the collection, whether they were interested or not. He learned to make beautiful jewellery with some of the rocks and proudly enjoyed showing off the pieces he had made.

When I moved from Kamloops to Vancouver in 1957 with my friend Marilyn, we lived in the Castle's basement with all the rocks for a short time. Dorothy cooked wonderful meals for us and the Castles were always fun to be around. (Marilyn eventually married one of the twin's friends from Burnaby.)

When Dorothy became ill and was placed in an extended care home, Henry was devastated. He faithfully visited her every day without fail and apparently always managed to keep the staff entertained. It was extremely difficult for Henry to cope when Dorothy died in 1989. This was the year of his eightieth birthday.

Dorothy endured much teasing through her years of marriage to Henry. One of his favourite tricks, when she dropped off for a nap in her chair, was to place an empty beer bottle on the table beside her and snap a photo. He found great humour in these photos and loved showing them to people.

It took a number of years for Henry to find the strength to actually put his house up for sale. He said that he never felt he had a home during his youth and this was his only real home. A few days after the property was sold in 1994, the new owner hired a crew to demolish the house. Henry drove there every day to see the proceedings. He sat in his truck across the street and watched every minute of his home being torn down.

It was apparently while Henry travelled around the coast to fish, after retiring, that he began to appreciate and be in touch with his Indian roots. He spent time visiting and making friends on the Capilano Reserve.

Many in our family thought of Henry as our own medicine man. He had a great knowledge of herbal and native cures for any type of condition. But nobody ever really knew when he was actually serious or was telling a story. He had that perpetual sparkle in his eyes.

Henry's daughter-in-law, Judy, wrote the following poem:

THE ROCKHOUND

I met an old man who collected rocks
He was 84 and sharp as a fox.

He remembered his jaunts through hill and dale
Every time I met him he would tell me a tale.

He took with him his wife and his son
He met with his friends and he drank some
rum.

They explored the caves, deserts and an old
creek bed
They sifted through the land wherever it led.

They looked for crystals, opals and gold
They sat around the fires and stories they told.

His stories filled me with wondrous delight
As he looked for his treasures at each different
site

Never knowing if there was anything to be
found
It didn't really matter to the old Rock Hound.

He filled his basement from ceiling to floor
He kept the valuables in a box behind the door.

He made jewellery out of many a precious gem
Of silver and gold for women and men.

He kept some for himself and wore them with
pride
He told some tall tales, but I knew he lied!

The house he built heard the babies cry
Saw them grow as time passed by.

His wife passed on to her favourite place
The Rock Hound looked around...he had too
much space.

It was time to move on, he put the house up for
sale
He changed his address for incoming mail.

He needed help to pack his stuff
I went to the basement....it was going to be
rough!

Every rock for him a memory dear
He'd tell me a tale and drop an invisible tear.

We looked at the cobwebs and the dust
The darkness, the old crates and all his stuff.

He said with a chuckle, "I sure had fun!"
He wouldn't have traded lives with anyone.

And that's when I knew he was a happy man
This...another stage in life's plan

I'll still see his smiles when he's around
And listen to the stories of that Indian Rock
Hound.

After Dorothy died, it was devastating for Henry to lose both Hopie and Ruth within five years. They all had that special Indian sense of humour and found great hilarity in calling each other by their Coqualeetza identification numbers.

Henry stayed close to his son, Herb, during his last years and met a lady friend, distantly related, who became his travelling companion. They travelled in his van all over the country, visiting and rock-hunting. I'll always remember seeing him jogging up my front stairs in his sneakers at the age of 86 after driving from Vancouver to Kamloops in his brand-new van. He had a head of dark hair, hardly a grey strand to be found. It took me by surprise when he asked me at that time for copies of the Coqualeetza Annuals in my possession. He sought and accomplished receiving his Indian status at the age of 85, after a number of years of endless red tape, and had plans to move to Popkum for his remaining years.

Henry died in his sleep in July 1998 at the age of eighty-nine. This was a shock to everyone since he seemed so extraordinarily healthy. Shortly before his death, he told Herb that the Black Crow had visited him. Although Herb didn't know what he meant, he knew it was not good.

When Henry's obituary was printed in the Vancouver paper, a woman phoned the family to extend her condolences because she remembered him so fondly as her milkman in the forties.

Dorothy and Henry
(date unknown)

August and Henry Castle,
1960s

Henry on rock
hunting trip,
early 1990s

Ruth   Henry   Hopie

Henry's 80th birthday party, 1989.
The last photo of the 3 Castles together.

Many came to Henry's funeral. One of his treasured rocks was given out to each person at the entrance door. The following poem was all that was printed on the memorial pamphlet.

Walk softly
follow my footsteps
'til we meet at Dawn.
When the storms close in
and the eyes cannot find the horizon
you may lose much.
Stay with your love for life
for it is the very blood
running through your veins.
As you pass through the years
you will find much calmness in your heart.
It is the gift of age,
and the colours of the fall
will be deep and rich.
If you let it happen.

-- Chief Dan George

~oo0oo~

Interviews

Following are ex-student interviews during the Coqualeetza Reunion in 1972:

Peter Minnabarriet

I only spent three years of my life at Coqualeetza. In my case I was sort of a guest student. I was originally a pupil at St. George's Residential School at Lytton but as there were no facilities for high school there, it was arranged that I attend high school in Sardis. I attended and completed my first year of high school at Coqualeetza and the following two years I commuted daily to Chilliwack High School while boarding at Coqualeetza. I graduated as a Junior Matric student at Chilliwack High School.

The few years I spent at Coqualeetza influenced the greater part of the rest of my life. Only those who have lived the life of a Coqualeetza student can understand and realize the impact that Coqualeetza has cast on their lives. Coqualeetza was the vehicle that was responsible for attaining a higher education which filled a gap to bridge one life style or cycle to another, the roots of which reshaped the destiny of many students.

We shouldn't allow Coqualeetza to become just a name or word as time goes by. We should erect a suitable plaque depicting the history and quote the school motto "*Vestigia Nulla Retrorsum,*" *No* backward Step.

I have tried to live by this motto all through my life – in my 41 years of railroading career and in my six years of army life, both here and overseas. On looking back I think this was quite a motto and I was very much impressed with it. I feel that I am not qualified to express any further impressions or observations, as most of my life was lived on the fringe of the true Indian culture, of which I now regret.

The Chilliwack Progress newspaper featured a story on the Coqualeetza reunion and interviewed several well-known ex-students. Following are several excerpts:

Senator Guy Williams

When asked to recall his four years at Coqualeetza (1919-1923), Senator Williams told The Progress, "I remember Chilliwack as a very small town with a very clannish soccer team. I still bear some of the scars from those soccer matches. They (the Chilliwack players) were men and we were boys but that didn't seem to make much difference." He also recalled Chilliwack as a "good place for a 10 cent show" and said that his years at the residential school gave him an opportunity to say yes and no and answer the important question, where am I going?"

Coqualeetza, he said, made a "fairly good contribution to the parts of this province where its students came from." And, in conclusion, he noted, "be sure you mention that Coqualeetza always had a heck of a good soccer team."

Senator Williams was appointed to the Upper Chamber in December of 1971. He was a member of the Native Brotherhood of B.C. for eleven years and, as Business Agent for three years, gained an overall knowledge of Native issues.

The Honourable Mr. Frank Calder

It was very sad for me when I learned that the school closed in 1940. I always felt they could have built a TB hospital elsewhere. Coqualeetza Residential School made a valuable contribution to the growth of this province." He added, "Graduates from the school have taken a wide spectrum of walks of life." He mentioned, for instance, that Basil

Robinson, a graduate of the school, was a Rhodes Scholar and is now deputy minister of Indian Affairs.

"I could fill a book with my memories from Coqualeetza," the minister of the crown said. "I came here when I was eight and a half years old and for 13 very important years Coqualeetza was my home."

And, like Senator Williams, Hon. Mr. Calder also emphasized the importance of sports at Coqualeetza. "We Indian kids were very shy and unsure of ourselves and sports such as soccer gave us an outlet and an opportunity to gain confidence."

He said the influence of non-Indian classmates of Chilliwack Senior Secondary School encouraged him to go on to UBC to further his studies and he concluded, "I think very often of Coqualeetza and the effect that it has had on my life. When I came here today. I couldn't help but have many, many memories. I only regret that we didn't start to have these reunions earlier."

The Honourable Frank Calder attended Coqualeetza Residential School from 1924 to 1937 and graduated from Chilliwack Senior Secondary School. In 1978, he celebrated 25 years in the Legislature. He ran for election for the CCF in 1941 and was the first Indian candidate ever to run and be elected in a B.C. election. He was the country's only Indian cabinet minister. He became president of the Nishga Tribal Council, which filed a suit against the provincial government in 1969 for title to land in northwestern B.C.'s Nass River Valley. This resulted in the current Nishga Treaty giving them self-government powers to manage their own affairs and remove them from the Indian Act.

Solomon Wilson

Mr. Wilson arrived at Coqualeetza Residential School in 1899. He told The Progress on Saturday, "When I got here, I couldn't say anything more than *yes* or *no* and my classmates used to translate for me. I never was much at learning, but what I did learn here (he left in 1904) helped me a lot. I never did learn how to write a letter but I could figure well and when I worked on the fishing boats, I handled thousands and thousands of dollars without any trouble."

Mr. Wilson, still remarkably healthy, told The Progress - "When I was here, I was the black sheep. Everything I did was wrong. I even got punished once for giving a girl a big king apple, without asking the teacher first."

Ruth and Delavina attended the opening of the Kwakiutl Museum on June 29, 1979 at Cape Mudge Village, Quadra Island, B.C. Following are some comments from ex-students who were present at the celebration. There were many more interviews planned which they were not able to do.

Sandy Argus

The old school, the dormitories and school house were cold. They had wooden sides but tent tops that didn't keep out the cold.

What were your jobs at Coqualeetza?

When I was small, I made beds and cleaned up the dormitories. When I was older, I looked after the cows, barns and pigs. Every Saturday morning, we scrubbed the whole kitchen and dining room. We baked the bread. Sometimes the bread was really good, sometimes it was sour, mushy and lumpy. The trouble with the bread was we had three ovens – you had to keep changing the bread around. One oven cooked the top, the other cooked the bottom. We baked 600 loaves at a time every few days.

Russ Modest

At the Archives we discovered that in 1915 Dr. Raley was already concerned about the children coping with returning to the reserves. *What did it do for you and what do you think it did for the children generally?*

I have mixed feelings about Coqualeetza. Now that I have matured, I look back and some of it I feel kind of unsure. While I was there, I felt there were so many restrictions. You couldn't even look at the girls' side or you were in trouble. After leaving Coqualeetza I felt deprived of an academic education. I can see Dr. Raley's point when he brought in vocational training, but I detested milking cows. I was more interested in an academic education. It seemed to me there was a muzzling, you didn't speak out of turn. But when I look back, I can see now the vocational training was useful. You know I built this home on my own. It was part of the training at school and for that reason I was able to handle a saw and tools. I just finished putting this porch on but we aren't quite finished. As little kids we were made acquainted with tools. Now they start at junior high level. I am thankful now what has been done for me.

One reason I wound up in Coqualeetza is that my parents had separated. Theirs was an arranged marriage. They weren't compatible so they separated. This raised hell with us because we were confused and caught in the middle. My mom took half of the kids and dad took the older ones and shipped us off to Coqualeetza. That is how I wound up in Coqualeetza. Otherwise I would never have gone because we were baptized as Roman Catholics. When my parents separated, my Dad went to the United Church and we were re-baptized.

How did you feel when you first went to Coqualeetza?

I hated it, being away from my family, not being able to speak my own language. At the age of nine I couldn't speak a word of English. When I arrived there, when someone spoke to me they could have been speaking Italian. They let Charlie Williams and others help me over the rough times. Within about six months you learned the fundamentals, enough to get you by in the classroom. What disturbed me the most was the diet, it was so different from home-cooked meals. Most of our meals at home had been fish or game.

But all in all, when I look back and talk to a good number of those having gone to Coqualeetza they say pretty much the same. They feel it has been a real education being in a place like that. They feel it prepared them for the change in life; we were caught in between. At least we have some inkling of what our kids are experiencing now, from the old traditional Indian lifestyle to the contemporary. I always felt that we were so far behind and we needed to catch up, and I was always saying to myself, let's go, let's go. You know it is not too many years ago on this reserve that we were able to get electricity. Until then most of the old people refused it. They felt that once you were connected you signed on the dotted line and you had to pay every month whether you could or not.

That is one outstanding thing to me, when I came out of Coqualeetza I experienced the change in lifestyle. I was disappointed and almost hostile to the lifestyle of my people because when I arrived back home, I had to pack water, heat it to take a bath. You couldn't push a button to switch the light on. You had to take the coal oil lamp, or gas lamp, clean it, fill it, etc. and I made a vow to myself that someday when I am able to, I'm going to have indoor plumbing, all the amenities that I became accustomed to in school. I think we were the fifth house on this whole reserve that got indoor plumbing. That is only about 20 years ago. I was able to do this through picking up books and from the learning experiences I had in Coqualeetza. I was able to pour cement, build my own chimney.

Speaking of books, did you use the school library?

Yes, I did. It got us accustomed to books. However, I was never really a bookworm. As a matter of fact I stayed away from the library purposely. I think I resented being cooped up. No, my interest in reading came when I was in the service. You were so far from home, no money, so I turned to the newspaper. At school, the library was situated more on the girls' side of the building. Also, I think the boys were too preoccupied with recreational sports like soccer and basketball. The boys played and played soccer and became excellent players, also at some other sports.

When I left school, I felt we were restricted too much. We had so many rules to obey. The only time I'll go to church now is for a wedding or a funeral. I went to church quite regularly shortly after leaving school, then I found that other people were not attending. Now when I look back on Sundays at Coqualeetza I remember rising early, washing, brushing my teeth and morning prayers. Then at 11 o'clock we attended the regular service, then the evening service. At the time I thought that a kid coming out of Coqualeetza was already half way to heaven, they can't get into trouble now.

Shortly after I came out of Coqualeetza I joined the army. I fitted in like a glove because there was no difference from school. I took orders, I polished my boots, behaved myself. I thought I was an ideal soldier. I was used to discipline. I was punctual and it seemed the attitude of the staff kind of rubbed off on me, "good old England." I sort of adopted that feeling – England is in trouble and I have to get over there and do something – so I volunteered at a very young age. I served four years. When I was heading out on the first troop train it stopped to back off the next rail for the next train to come in. I was looking out and saw Wesley Sam. I met a number of boys I knew from school on our way to England.

During the war I was in Italy for just about a year and a half in combat. When I left there and went back to England there was some relief but I think the dependency to alcohol during combat was still there. The alcohol gave us false courage. Upon arriving home that problem increased. I am happy to say that I have overcome that problem. I stayed in AA meetings for over 20 years. I used to say, if it wasn't for those damn buggers; sergeants in the army, the warrant officers, and Mr. Pirie at school. I blamed them all.

But all in all I've had a good hard life. The great Lord can take me away any time, I am fairly satisfied. I've raised a family. But I still have some resentments, particularly about the land claims. I used to hear my grandfather and dad speak of the land claims, about the white man taking over our land and giving us their religion. There has got to be a reason for this – this was my maternal grandfather's reasoning. They are changing you, preparing you along with the younger ones, softening you up to a complete takeover. It has almost come to that now. This is the only resentment I have now, governments.

Wesley Sam

At Coqualeetza I learned about B.C. and other communities, their habits and culture from students coming from other reserves. I would not have had the opportunity in a local public school.

We have done a lot of church work, Myra and I. I do believe that residential schools provided us with culture and religion and a wide variety of programs because the facilities were there. The teachers and the expertise were there. We learned to work together.

I find that Myra and I, having the same background and same outlook, has made a solid marriage, this is one of the advantages. We could more easily agree on how to raise the children. There are other couples like Mike and Josephine, Nora and Art – they have brought up good families. This also has helped in developing our community and this reflects back to Coqualeetza.

We were really fortunate in this fact. I would not have had the same grounds with which to build upon. As a matter of fact, our Coqualeetza training is quite superior right today. People could not believe we had this type of training. The young people today have the advantage of knowing the language when they go to school, we had to learn to speak English before we could start classes. I was able to become familiar with many things there that I could never have done at home.

Ruby Hovell Wilson

In our Indian language, we have the words "Our Heavenly Father." We know there is a creator bigger than you and me. They (the missionaries) crushed the Indian culture because they didn't understand. Why did they talk about us as heathens and savages?

Like the Hamatsha - the magicians of the secret society. They went into hiding in the woods until the day of the Potlatch. They went into the woods so they could learn how to live outside of the normal society. Not all the people knew about the secret society, just a select few. They would choose a victim ahead of time. The day of the Potlatch the Hamatsha would grab the victim and bite him on the neck, and when he moved away blood would ooze. It was really from the berries in his mouth. The Hamatsha had to be strong as he lifted the victim aloft and danced, drawing closer and closer to the fire which was burning. It looked like the victim landed in the fire and then disappeared but he actually didn't. The sparks would fly, you smell the cloth, then the burning flesh. The climax of this act is, maybe a few hours later, or even days later, the victim comes walking in the front door wearing the same clothes as he was wearing when he was thrown into the fire.

When the missionaries saw this, they believed people were actually thrown into the fire. The trick was, a hole and a passage were dug that would go from one house to another. Only a few from the society knew how this was done. The victim was hidden this way until the appropriate time for him to appear. The passage was just under the fire. There was someone in the passage with a stick and he created the sparks in the fire above which helped to hide the act. He also did the screaming for the victim.

There was always a dramatic build-up to the climax; this was true of the speeches and dancing. So, when the victim appeared a week later, it was pure drama. When you watch the magicians today put a victim in a box and cut her in half, we don't know how they do it. Just like the secret society. Even the people didn't know how it was done. So the government got into it because they thought the Indians were wild. We believed that the missionaries came with preconceived ideas.

~oo0oo~

Sources

Barman, Jean. "Lost Opportunity: All Hallows School for Indian and White Girls 1884-1920." *B.C. Historical News*, vol 2. Spring 1989. [Source: B.C. Archives]

Barman. Jean, "Separate and Unequal: Indian and White Girls at All Hallows School. 1884-1920." *Indian Education in Canada*. vol 1. Vancouver: UBC Press. 1986. [Source: B.C. Archives]

Bjerky, Irene. *Christmas at All Hallows :Yale 1902-1932.* [Source: Yale & District Historical Society]

Carlson, Keith Thor, editor. *You Are Asked to Witness*: *The Stô:lô in Canada's Pacific* Coast *History.* Chilliwack: Stó:lō Heritage Trust, 1997. [Source: Chilliwack Archives Acct. No. 2001 32. Contact David Schaeppe – Sonny McHalsie. Stó:lō offices]

Coqualeetza Commencement Annuals: 1924, 1928, 1929, 1930, 1931, 1932, 1934

Gordon, Leigh. *Young Ladies Go to Yale, B.C. for Refinement.* [Source: Yale & District Historical Society]

Haig-Brown, Celia *Resistance and Renewal, Surviving the Indian Residential School.* Vancouver: Arsenal Pulp Press, 2006.

McFadden, Isobel. *Living by Bells: A narrative of five schools in British Columbia, 1874-1970.* Toronto?: Committee on Education for Mission and Stewardship, United Church of Canada, 1971.

McIvor, Dorothy Matheson. *Coqualeetza: Vestigia Nulla Retrorsum (No Backward Step).* Blue Door Publishing, 2001. [Source: Chilliwack Archives]

Mission I Canada. *COMBO*, summer 1973. [Newspaper]

Native Brotherhood of British Columbia (NBBC). *The Native Voice*, February, 1948.

Raibmon, Paige. "A New Understanding of Things Indian: George Raley's Negotiation of the Residential School Experience". *B.C. Studies,* No. 110, summer 1996. [Source: UBC Library]

Raley, Rev. George Henry, George Henry Raley fonds - PR-0465. Victoria: B.C. Archives. ca. 1883-1957. [Correspondence, speeches, research notes, articles]

Scott, Robert C. "Foundations and Progress" [Article]

"Short Rules for Comfort at Home." [Source: Yale & District Historical Society]

Smith, Ruth. Personal collection: notes, interview recordings and personal photos.

The Chilliwack Progress. Editions: October 1919, October 1924, November 24, 1948, October 25, 1972, August 23, 1978. Chilliwack B.C.. [Newspaper archives URL: https://theprogress.newspapers.com]

The Vancouver Daily Province, October 1924, February 13 1957, December 15, 1972

The Vancouver Sun, June 13, 1969

Wallace, Claire. Personal letter, October 16, 1948 [Radio talk show]

Western Methodists Recorder, August 1988

Wood, Jody. "Coqualeetza Legacies of Land Use," in *A Stó:lo-Coast Salish Historical Atlas.* Keith Thor Carlson, editor. Vancouver: Douglas & McIntyre / Chilliwack: Stó:lō Heritage Trust, 2001, pp74-5. [Source: Chilliwack Archives Acc. No. 2001 32]

About the Author

Sandra **Baker** retired from business in the early 1990's after living in the U.S.A., England and Calgary for over 20 years. She and her daughter later moved to the Kamloops area to be close to family and to care for her mother, Ruth. During that time, she learned more about her family's historical past and felt compelled to write the Castle family's life stories. She is now living back in Vancouver enjoying watching her granddaughter grow up.

Hopie and Ruth outside Coqualeetza, 1920